W9-BLV-217

"[An] elegant, painful memoir... l up to a vivid, often brutal image." —*Publishers Weekly*

"A poetic journey into the expansive Chicano heart ... This book shines with genius." —Rudolfo Anaya

"Urrea is not simply a great writer and a wonderful storyteller; he is completely enamored with words and language—not so much as tools of the trade but as life's sustenance." —*Booklist* (starred review)

"Author, thinker and word provocateur, Urrea has become one of the most clear and articulate interpreters of the border region.... He cuts through the thicket of language and cultural contradictions, offering up both humorous looks at his life and troubling memories." —*San Diego Union-Tribune*

"Lyrical and often painfully funny snapshots of a family damaged as much by alcohol and poverty as by the push and pull of cultures in conflict." —*Dallas Morning News*

"*Nobody's Son* is an engaging reflection of life, conflict and spirit. It shows how Urrea applies lessons learned to his own development in his continued search for self." —*Rocky Mountain News*

"Colorful narratives of family history, boyhood vignettes and social commentary that are at once funny, sad, tough and tender." —*Arizona Republic*

"The cross-cultural conflicts of Urrea's youth are grist for his literary mill, and he writes about them in a compelling, vivid style laced with self-deprecating humor. His love of the English language—his second language—is as obvious as his mastery of it."—*Christian Century*

"Energetic and darkly humorous memoirs ... about the challenge of explaining a dual identity, a task he accomplishes with passion and understanding." —*Library Journal*

Camino del Sol

a Latina and Latino literary series

The University of Arizona Press

Luis Alberto Urrea

nobody's son

notes from an american life

Tucson

First paperbound printing 2002
The University of Arizona Press
© 1998 Luis Alberto Urrea
All rights reserved

Library of Congress Cataloging-in-Publication Data
Urrea, Luis Alberto.
Nobody's son: notes from an American life / Luis Alberto Urrea.
p. cm. — (Camino del sol)
ISBN 0816518653 (cloth: acid-free, archival-quality paper)
ISBN 0816522707 (pbk: acid-free, archival-quality paper)
1. Urrea, Luis Alberto—Biography. 2. Mexican American
authors—20th century—Biography. 3. Southwestern States—
Social life and customs. 4. Mexican Americans—Social life and
customs. 5. Mexico—Social life and customs. I. Title. II. Series.
PS3571.R74 Z47 1998
818'.5409—ddc21
[B]   98-8924

Manufactured in the United States of America on acid-free, archival-
quality paper.

17 16 15 14 13   10 9 8 7 6

For Cinderella,
  who brought back the words.

For Jonna and Steve,
  who kept the faith.

contents

acknowledgments

My bride, Cinderella Urrea. Jonna Faulkner and Steve Rossman. Darrell Bourque, Brian Andrew Laird—true friends and fine readers. David Thomson.

Mr. Ernest Gaines, good neighbor and our own Neruda.
Martha Moutray. Naomi Horii. Judith Allen.
Robert Boswell. Gary Holthaus. Shawn Phillips.
My uncle, Douglas White—Oglala Lakota Medicine Man.
César González.

Finally, thanks to the Urrea children, mi familia. Their stories are more wonderful and terrible than mine.

Y gracias, Teresita Urrea.

Part One

Nobody's Son

"You're in big trouble when you got to apologize for being yourself."

—Cajun folk saying

I

My mom said, "I'm so sick of your God-damned Mexican bullshit!" I was in bed with my wife at the time. It was 7:30 in the morning. My wife was white. So was my mother.

Apparently, the issue of my identity was troubling Mom. She was a good Republican. She tended to work up a good cuss when she was beyond her limit of endurance. I must have come to represent a one-man wave of illegal aliens to her as she sipped her coffee and looked out at a tender New England dawn.

I had finally gotten away from the border. I was teaching writing, at Harvard no less. She saw this development as being due to the force of her own will. That's the GOP for you, I'd say in our frequent and spirited political squabbles—taking credit for someone else's achievements while demonizing their ethnicity. (Did you know that *squabble* is a Scandinavian word? So what, you ask? Just keep it in mind, that's all.)

I was still being called Mexican, Chicano, Hispanic, Latino, Mexican American, Other. These Ivy-League types were taking my name seriously. It drove my mother to distraction.

She barged through the door shouting anti-Mexican rhetoric. Whither goest Mom goest the nation.

We had a miniature Proposition 187 anti-immigration rally right there in my bedroom.

"You are *not* a Mexican!" she cried. "Why can't you be called *Louis* instead of *Luis*?"

Go, Mom.

"Louis *Woodward* or Louis *Dashiell.* One of *my* names. I'm warning you—someday, they're going to come for you, and you'll be sorry."

They.

I've been on the lookout for those scoundrels all my life. So has much of my family. (When I mention my family, I mean Mexicans. The Americans were held at bay by my mother for reasons I only later understood. It turns out she was ashamed of the Mexicans. "They spit on the floor," she insisted, though I never saw my *abuelita* hawk up a big one and splash it in the corner. If your mama's saying it, it must be true.) Many of my relatives were afraid of the border patrol. Others were afraid of the Mexican government. Still others were afraid of Republican white people and Democratic black people. Cops. And perhaps my white relatives back East were afraid of all these things, too. But mostly, I got to thinking, they must have been scared of me. I was one of them, but I was also one of *them*.

They.

"They," Wendell Berry writes, "will want you to kneel and weep / and say you should have been like them."

It's a poem called "Do Not Be Ashamed." I read it whenever I'm called upon to give a commencement speech at college graduations. It's not a political poem. It's not a liberal or conservative poem. It's a human poem.

Most students seem to understand what Berry's talking about.

He goes on to say:

And once you say you are ashamed,
reading the page they hold out to you,
then such light as you have made
in your history will leave you.
They will no longer need to pursue you.
You will pursue them, begging forgiveness.

They.

You can almost see thought bubbles above the students' heads as they listen. *Honkies,* some are thinking. *Liberals,* and *minorities,* and *commies.* And certainly *666* and *the Antichrist* bubble about up in the air: *Hispanics, Yankees, blacks, queers. Democrats. Women. Men.*

My mother thought: *Mexicans.*

My father, a Mexican, thought: *gringos.*

I, for one, think *They* are the ones with the words. You know, the Words. The ones they called my dad and me—like *wetback. Spic. Beaner. Greaser. Pepper-belly. Yellow-belly. Taco-bender. Enchilada-breath.*

That was my wife's phrase. She thought it was cute. She's gone now.

So is my mom.

"Dad?" I said. "What's a greaser?"

He used to tell me I was no *God-damned gringo.* I was, however, white. *Speak Spanish, pendejo!* was a common cry when I spoke some unacceptable English phrase. Utterly forbidden English in our house included many taboos, among them: *my old man* (he was sure this was disrespectful and implied he wasn't a virile young thing); *big daddy* (he was certain this meant big penis); *you're kidding* (another disrespect, suggesting he didn't tell the truth at all times—he didn't); *easy rider* (he thought this meant a man married to a whore); *chicano* (from chicanery).

His only word for *them* was *gringo.* He didn't see it as all that bad. He said it came from the Mexican-American War. The pop hit the American soldiers sang in those days was "Green Grow the Lilacs." Green grows/*gringos.* It seemed altogether benign compared to yellow bellies.

I had been called "greaser" by the son of a retired Navy petty officer in my new, all-white neighborhood. We had fled from the ethnic cleansing taking place in Shelltown, California, to which we had hurried from Tijuana. I couldn't quite fathom the name. Surely I wasn't greasy? But I *felt* greasy. And the vivid image of grease, of some noxious *Mexican* grease, collided in my mind with the word "wetback." And suddenly I was certain that my back was wet with grease. A grease I couldn't see. I had an image in my mind of the back of my shirt soaked through with cooking oil and sticking to me, glistening sickeningly in the sun. Everybody could see the grease drooling down my spine. Except me.

My father was whiter than my mother. If he had become an American citizen, he would have voted for Nixon. Twice. Most Mexican immigrants—both "legal" and "illegal"— would vote Republican if given a chance, except the Republicans scare them, so they're forced to support the Clintons and Carters of this nation. It has been estimated that by 2050, Latinos will be the majority population of the world. Not only will America be "brown," but it will also be the home of the new Democrats. The Institutional Revolutionary Catholic Democratic Party ticket led by Edward James Olmos will sweep the elections. The paradigm will shift, as they say: the bogeyman will become the *chupacabras*. Bullfights at the county fair. Baja California will be the fifty-first state. The Buchanan Brigade Aryan Militia will mount an offensive in the Malibu Hills, holding nineteen gardeners and twelve nannies hostage. NASA will land the first lowrider on the moon. Just watch.

"Greaser," my father replied.

I believe he had prepared himself for this. On our first

day in the neighborhood, he'd been chased out of our driveway by an irate white man. You don't spend two decades living as a Mexican guest of Southern California without becoming fully aware of the genocidal urge that percolates in the human heart.

Dad transformed before my eyes into a college lecturer.

"During the Americans' westward expansion," he intoned, "the settlers traveled in covered wagons. When they reached the West—Arizona, Texas, California—they often needed repair work done on their wagons after such a long hard trip. A large part of this work consisted of *greasing* the axles, which had dried out. The only ones who had the skill to fix the wagons were Mexicans. Mexicans greased the axles. You see? *Greasers.* So when they call you that, hold your head up. It's a badge of honor. We helped build America."

He's gone now, too.

The last time I was interviewed by the Mexican press, I was in Mexico City, the self-appointed home of all true Mexicans. I was startled to find out that I was not a true Mexican. I was any number of things: I was an American, I was "just" a Chicano, I was a *norteño* (which, in Mexico City, is like saying you're one of the Mongol horde). I was lauded for speaking Spanish "just like" a Mexican, or chided for having what amounted to a cowboy accent. That I was born in Tijuana didn't matter a bit: Tijuana, I was informed, is no-man's-land. Mexicans don't come from Tijuana. Tijuanans come from Tijuana.

That I was an American citizen was apparently a *faux pas*. That I wrote in English was an insult. That I was blue-eyed, however, allowed me to pass for Mexican high society.

I will say this for Mexico City, though: people in La Capital have perfect manners. For all its travails and crises, Mexico City is the most civil city I've ever visited. Imagine a city where a cabbie returns your tip to you because you've paid him too much for his services. Imagine this same city reporting a stunning 700 assaults every day.

In the great museum, you can see a famous Aztec mask. One half of it is a smiling face. The other half is a skull.

I was told by the editor of the newspaper to be out of town by the time the interview appeared. Someone somewhere decided that what I had to say was somehow dangerous. I thought this was a joke. Then an editor took me to the foyer where several of the paper's reporters had been executed. *All I'm saying*, I protested, *is that poor people should be treated with respect.* She lit a cigarette and said, *Be out of town.*

Things that seemed perfectly clear to me turned confusing and opaque.

In the interview, I offered the often-quoted comment from *By the Lake of Sleeping Children* that I, as a son of the border, had a barbed-wire fence neatly bisecting my heart. The border, in other words, ran through me. The journalist said, "Aha!" and scribbled with real vigor.

When the article came out, however, the comment had

been transformed. I'm still not sure what it means. It said: "If you were to cut Urrea's heart open, you would find a border patrol truck idling between his ribs."

I was going to write, "Meanwhile, back home . . ." But where is home? Home isn't just a place, I have learned. It is also a language. My words not only shape and define my home. Words—not only for writers—*are* home. Still, where exactly is that?

Jimmy Santiago Baca reminds us that "Hispanics" are immigrants in our own land. By the time Salem was founded on Massachusetts Bay, any number of Urreas had been prowling up and down the Pacific coast of our continent for several decades. Of course, the Indian mothers of these families had been here from the start. But manifest destiny took care of us all—while we greased the wheels.

Them wagons is still rollin'.

I saw a hand-lettered sign on television. It was held up by a woman in stretch pants and curlers, and it said: America For Americans. A nearby man held up a sign exhorting the universe to speak English or go home.

The official language of the United States.

Well, sure. We speak English and, apparently, Ebonics. I want to call Chicano slang Aztonics while we're at it. *Orale,* Homes—we down, *¿qué no?* Simón, *vato*—let's trip out the *rucas* of the school board, *ese! Ese torcido rifa, locos!*

It's all English. Except for the alligator, which is a Spanish word. Lariat, too, is a Spanish word.

In fact, here's a brief list, in no particular order. It might help you score points in a trivia parlor game someday. All words borrowed from Spanish:

.   Chaps
Savvy
Palaver
Hoosegow
Palomino
Coyote
Pinto
Marijuana
Vamoose
Stampede
Buckaroo
Adobe
Saguaro
Rodeo
Ranch
Rancher
Patio
Key (as in Florida Keys)
Florida
Sarsaparilla
Navajo
Nevada
Machete
Texas
Alfalfa
Bonanza
Bronco

Calaboose
Canyon
Colorado
Fandango
Foofaraw
Guacamole
Hackamore
Beef jerky
Lasso
Abalone
Vanilla
Chocolate
Cigar

For example. Perfectly acceptable English. Nary an Aztonic word in sight.

You don't believe me about beef jerky, do you? I find it a little hard to believe, my own self. What's more American than a hunk of jerky? Cowboys, rednecks, crackers, wrestlers, mountain men gnaw away on planks of jerked beef!

Winfred Blevins, in the marvelous *Dictionary of the American West*, notes: "The word is an Americanized version of the Spanish term for jerked meat, *charqui.*"

I don't know what we're going to do. Forget about purifying the American landscape, sending all those ethnic types packing back to their homelands. Those illegal humans. (A straw-hat fool in a pickup truck once told my Sioux brother

Duane to go back where he came from. "Where to?" Duane called. "South Dakota?")

The humanoids are pretty bad, but how will we get rid of all those pesky foreign *words* debilitating the United States?

Those Turkish words (like *coffee*). Those French words (like *maroon*). Those Greek words (like *cedar*). Those Italian words (like *marinate*). Those African words (like *marimba*).

English! It's made up of all these untidy *words,* man. Have you noticed?

Native American (*skunk*), German (*waltz*), Danish (*twerp*), Latin (*adolescent*), Scottish (*feckless*), Dutch (*waft*), Caribbean (*zombie*), Nahuatl (*ocelot*), Norse (*walrus*), Eskimo (*kayak*), Tatar (*horde*) words! It's a glorious *wreck* (a good old Viking word, that).

Glorious, I say, in all of its shambling mutable beauty. People daily speak a quilt work of words, and continents and nations and tribes and even enemies dance all over your mouth when you speak. The tongue seems to know no race, no affiliation, no breed, no caste, no order, no genus, no lineage. The most dedicated Klansman spews the language of his adversaries while reviling them.

It's all part of the American palaver and squawk.

Seersucker: Persian.

Sandalwood: Sanskrit.

Grab a dictionary. It's easy. You at home—play along.

The $64,000 question for tonight: What the hell are we

speaking? What language (culture, color, race, ethnicity) is this anyway? Who are we?

Abbott: Aramaic.

Yo-yo: Philippino.

Muslin: Iraqi.

Yogurt: Turkish.

I love words so much. Thank God so many people lent us theirs or we'd be forced to point and grunt. When I start to feel the pressure of the border on me, when I meet someone who won't shake my hand because she has suddenly discovered I'm half Mexican (as happened with a landlady in Boulder), I comfort myself with these words. I know how much color and beauty we Others really add to the American mix.

My advice to anyone who wants to close the border and get them Messkins out is this: *don't dare start counting how many of your words are Latin, Baby.*

America—there's a Mexican in the woodpile.

II

Poor Old Ma.

That's what she called herself. She'd sign letters, "Your Poor Old Ma." She was anything but rustic. It amused her *New Yorker* wit to be seen as Ma Kettle among the California hicks and savages. If she'd had her way, she would have worn white gloves every day, and I would have been called Lewis, and I would have called her "Mother Dear."

Her name was Phyllis. (A Greek word, don't you know. It means "the green branch.") She married my dad, Alberto (an Old English name—Aethelberht meaning "noble, brilliant"), in San Francisco's city hall. It was sometime in the late forties or early fifties. My mother had, she often said, "never even *seen* a Mexican." (A Nahuatl word, the ancient name of the Aztec tribe, Mexica.) My father was not only blond and blue-eyed, but he was in uniform and a devil on the dance floor. Even though it was a Mexican uniform, my mother was a fool for that military cut, having served long and dangerous years in Europe during the war. Her heroes remained soldiers, men in her eyes brave and noble and almost unbearably touching. She had seen enough men die and suffer to make of each uniform a small haunting. (Haunt: Old French.)

Alberto was on the presidential staff of Mexico. He had a lot of gold buttons, a couple of medals, and captain's stripes. So did she.

He lived in the presidential palace in Mexico City. He drove a black Cadillac with the number two on the plates. (Número uno, of course, was the president's black Cadillac—despots have always liked a long black car.) Dad spent his free hours zooming over the mountains to Cuernavaca on a huge military Harley. He had access to the president's train, and he regularly flew in the president's DC-3. He had an aunt in San Francisco, and he flew there on occasion to buy jazz and swing 78s.

He tried to look like Erroll Flynn; she looked (to him) like Merle Oberon.

The fact of them was as unlikely then as the fact of myself seems to me now.

It is part of our job as writers to betray the dead. Still, there are certain details best left untold. I don't know if you believe in ghosts (Old English) or not. But lately, I feel wraiths (Scottish) hovering over my shoulder as I write. I will give you as much of the story (Greek) as I can. I want to tell you about them. Phyl and Al, though, want to keep some of it to themselves. (Them and they: Old Norse.)

I often wonder if the fact of my mother's life didn't trouble my father in mysterious ways. After all, she'd been to war, and he hadn't. My mother had done something much more macho than my dad ever managed to do. Though his story was by no means bland, as we'll see.

But first I'll tell you about the green branch that was my mother.

She came from Staten Island when Staten Island still had villages and bucolic woods. She was from the village of Richmond. Her family was partially Virginian—Woodwards—who boasted of a plantation in the recent past. Slaves.

When she wasn't lost in the Staten Island woods, visiting families with such awesomely alien names (to me) as "the Van Oppens" (she still had Leonard Van Oppen's faded poems in her trunk—they seemed like letters from F. Scott Fitzgerald), she was in Mattituck, Long Island. There, she was part of a tribe of "terrible" (always said fondly) boy cousins who called her "Gator." They used to hang off the sides of side-tracked boxcars as the morning express shot through, bare inches from their backs.

My mother's mother, the monumentally difficult Louise Woodward, sold antiques in Manhattan. One of her clients was John Steinbeck, who insisted that nobody there recognize him or say his last name. One of her uncles drank beer often with Einstein, but he only knew him as "Al." Eccentrics surrounded my mother. Grannie Effie dressed up in Indian garb and communed with plants, for example. And Auntie Jeanne was "the first woman up the Amazon." I assume they meant the first *white* woman up the Amazon. Auntie Jeanne was also known for hiding her important documents between her voluminous breasts. And, finally, there was "Auntie Piddle-Maker," an old Victorian who stood in the corner of the garden during picnics and smiled as a small puddle ran out from under the edge of her long dress.

In spite of a rich cast of characters, and my mother's endless hilarity over them, I can't imagine it was a happy childhood. Mom boasted constantly of being alone all through her childhood. "I didn't need anyone, dear boy," she'd say. "I didn't need this constant stimulation you seem to need. I made my own stimulation!" Once, my mother confessed darkly, she'd had to jump out of a second-story window to escape a Hungarian stepfather. She fell into a snowbank, then walked in the dark across the woods to someone's house. She was maddeningly unclear about what had happened, either before or after her leap. But it sounded plenty stimulating.

Once, she giggled, she'd saved up her money and bought a ticket on a Ford tri-motor airplane. She flew to West Virginia to see some relatives. She was twelve. Her mother didn't notice she was gone for two days.

After an untidy divorce from her first husband, my mother joined the Red Cross and sailed across the Atlantic on a troop transport to take part in World War II. She drove around battlefields making coffee and doughnuts. She was sitting in a bathtub in London when a buzz bomb went overhead, and the engine cut out, and it fell. She held the hands of flamethrower victims in a MASH tent. She hid in a farmhouse all night as German tanks rumbled past, not one hundred yards from the back wall. She entered Buchenwald with George Patton's troops and took ghastly photographs I was forbidden to see.

And then Mom was hurt.

She and two Red Cross pals were driving a Jeep near the front. I don't know where they were, though I suspect they were in Germany. The women had been serving coffee all day and were in a hurry to get back to base camp. I never knew who was driving.

They were in blackout conditions, so the headlights of the Jeep were taped down to small slits. The light was dim at best, less than the light thrown by parking lights today. It was getting late, and they were in mountains. The road was familiar to them, so the driver was taking the turns pretty fast.

I imagine them at the head of a ghostly train of dust,

their hair flying, the laughter a bit too loud, almost daring the snipers to get them. Laughing in the face of the ever-hungry death that surrounded them. One of the women was named Jill, and I can imagine my mother calling her "Jilly" and "dear girl." The night was getting chill. The trees, ragged negative spaces around them in the dark, smelled heady and beautiful after a day full of the smells of smoke, mud, blood, terror.

What they didn't know was that a mortar round had taken out the middle of the lane on a turn. The driver hit the crater full speed. The Jeep became airborne, and all three women were catapulted over the edge of the cliff.

She never knew how long they were down there.

She used to tell me she'd awakened to the sound of screaming. She was on her hands and knees in mud. She was crawling in the blackness, trying to find the screamer. The mud was actually a pond made of her own blood. And then she realized she herself was screaming.

I realize now, when I'm trying to tell you, that I don't know where the Jeep went—if it exploded, or tumbled, or stayed on the road, or even if it came down the slope on top of them. And I don't know what happened to the "girls." It never occurred to me to ask. Though later, in other stories, there was a "dear Jill" who vanished over the edge of a cliff and was never found.

My mother's leg was nearly severed. It was cut loose and bleeding wildly. The scar disfigured her leg for the rest of her life. You never saw my mom in shorts. She was never able to drive after the wreck. She grew unreasonably fearful of cars, especially in the mountains. And there was no way, for some reason, she would allow you to drive her over a bridge. You could only get Phyl over such barriers as the Hudson River or the San Francisco Bay with a good shot of Baileys Irish Cream.

When their marriage became a long chess game of hate, my father would turn our Sunday drives into small torture sessions. He'd make our '49 Ford take Cuyamaca Mountain's curves a hair too fast, and my Poor Old Ma would frantically stomp her foot on the phantom brake, and my father would laugh at her. "Please, Papa," she'd mutter.

"Jesus Christ, Feliciana," he'd reply, blowing smoke through his nostrils. "We're only going forty-five!"

Feliciana was what he made of Phyllis, a name utterly alien to a Mexican. Most of the relatives called her "La Pillips." My dad's name for her roughly meant "happy woman." One of those tawdry little ironies writers pay a nickel for.

Sometime late in that catastrophic night, Mom became aware of flashlights zigzagging down the cliff toward her. She tried to stifle her cries, for she couldn't know what fate was descending. She was certain the Nazis had found her and would finish her when a light hit her full in the eyes and a good old New York G.I. yelled, "Jesus, it's goyls!" (*Goyls*, my mother always said, remembering this midnight saint and giggling. It never failed to make her laugh—the real, tinkling laugh, the happiness bell she so seldom rang. For the rest of her life, this forgotten soldier's accent turned her into a delighted six-year-old.)

The soldiers dressed her wounds. Again, imagination has failed me until this moment, when I write it. What was the scene? How many men from that patrol bent over her, cut her clothes away? My mother, with her actress looks, ripped and bleeding and naked in the tender hands of these armed men. What did she feel? Did her modesty protest? Was she embarrassed? Did my mother cry?

And the soldiers, out on killing business, suddenly transformed to sweaty angels. What a scene it must have been. I can hear them trying to calm her as they constructed some sort of stretcher and hoisted her to their shoulders. Their rough and dirtied hands holding her steady as they struggled up the slope with her. And the long and mysterious journey in their care. Did they find a truck? Did they carry her all the way?

My mother, bouncing through the night, bleeding her life away into the filthy undershirts of unnamed, faceless warriors.

Six weeks in a hospital tent. The field surgeons stitched her back together. Whenever I watch MASH, I see my mother.

Once, as she lay in her bed, the surgeons came for her. Two men had been using a flamethrower, and it had exploded, cooking them alive. They were in an adjacent tent, and there was nothing anyone could do. The surgeons thought the only one who could bring such burned men comfort as they died was a woman.

She was carried into the tent. She said the men were horribly blackened, stickmen, with their arms raised as if in praise. And when the others set her down beside the reeking cots, she broke down crying. The burned man nearest her broke open charred lips and whispered words of comfort to her. She took his wooden hand and held it, and he told her, "It's all right, lady. It's not so bad." She was guilty for years about crying. But I think it was a gift. I think the suffering appreciate the chance to comfort others.

Those soldiers had done terrible things with their flamethrowers. And their weapons had turned on them and brought a fearsome retribution on them. "Nobody wins," my mother told me about war. "Nobody wins a war." But those two men died lying side by side with her, holding her hand, perhaps smelling her perfume, drinking her woman's voice in shaky gulps, and using their last smoky breaths to try to ease her suffering.

Perhaps they were her only true loves. Perhaps they were her own personal angels. There seems to be a terrible grace in this story. When she finally died, perhaps she was searching for their faces—hoping to find them new and young again, gleaming and unsullied, fresh as a field of snow.

These scenes weren't the only ones that haunted her. There was the night the Russian troops entered a village where she was bivouacked, and the G.I.'s had to hide the Red Cross women because the Russians were raping any women they found. There was the period when she was stationed at a B-17 base and watched as the big wounded planes came in and exploded. There was the time she was ferried across the channel on a B-17; I have the picture.

She sits with her eyes clamped shut, praying for mercy. She said the airmen laughed at her all the way across.

There was the time she partied near the front with an artillery unit, and, tipsy on champagne, she pulled the lanyards on the big guns and sent heavy shells into the German lines. In my idiotic childhood innocence I cried, "You *killed* people?"

She just looked away.

"I don't know," she said. "I suppose I might have . . ."

Then she would stare out our window at the sad yellow ghetto lawn.

And there was Buchenwald.

She wouldn't talk about it. Not much anyway. She did say that she was ashamed to be taking pictures, and her shame finally forced her to stop. She said that tractors moved logjams of naked bodies around, and she didn't know what they were at first, since nobody could understand a tall hill of corpses at first glance. You just weren't prepared for such a sight.

Like many soldiers, she kept a clutch of atrocity pictures. She didn't know what to do with them. She couldn't bear to throw them away. That would be like killing those innocent people again. But she couldn't bear to look at them either. And she didn't want me to see them.

She had a footlocker in which she kept her World War II stuff. It was stenciled with her first married name: McLaughlin. In it were captured German items, pictures, dispatches, an army jacket with 7th Army patches on it. A picture of Hitler. A picture of Churchill and Eisenhower getting into a car. Scores of B-17 portraits. And the forbidden envelope of holocaust photos.

I remember opening the trunk and finding them when she was at work. The dead skeletons are some of my first memories. The pile of babies that had been used by the guards for target practice—neatly stacked, as if the crime would have been making a mess, not killing them. The impossibly thin corpses lying in strange positions on the gray earth. Humans made into abstracts by an unknowable process.

"I saw 10,000 die," Mom once told me.

All of them came to her room at night and made her whimper and cry out. I listened to my mother scream through her sleep every night.

"Don't ever touch me in my sleep," she'd warn. "You'll kill me."

Sometimes I'd stand in her doorway and pray that she'd stop kicking and crying "No."

After the war, she sought solace in the beauty of San Francisco.

It must have seemed like springtime to her. She was free of the war, free of the marriage, free of her complicated family in New York. She was making good money as a jewelry buyer for a major department store, and she had teamed up with fellow Red Cross "doughnut girls" and other bon vivants. Those were heady days—San Francisco coming alive with the terrible Beats, with the postwar energy that rippled up and down the hills. And Poor Old Ma, never one to do things by half measures, decided the bohemian life was for her: she rented a houseboat in Sausalito.

How could Alberto Urrea Murray not have seemed part of the charm? (Yes, Murray. Even on my Mexican side, I'm Irish.) Phyllis was English and Scottish and some Hungarian. Her ancestors were plantation owners in Virginia—great grannie remembered hanging a "yard negro" for being caught in the house. ("House" being Old English, and "Negro" being Spanish. What language is this? What is a Hispanic?) He was five-foot-seven, wore size seven shoes, had sparkling blue eyes and a charming accent. He didn't want an accent, but if he had to have one, his would be patterned after Ricardo Montalban's or Gilbert Roland's. None of that Desi Arnaz Cuban mush-mouth talk for Al.

My mother thought he was European. Perhaps she imagined him on a handsome *hacienda,* surrounded by singing *charros* and palomino horses. The closest she had gotten to a Mexican before my father was watching *Zorro.*

Their story was a good one.

Phyl was at a garden party somewhere in the city. Apparently, due to her friendships and her standing in the retail community, she attended many fancy do's. This particular party was attended by a curious mix of Latinos—film actors, businessmen, and ambassadors' staffers. And Mom, looking sleek in her black dress and white pearls, her gloves and her pillbox hat with the vapor-thin veil, her Tiffany brooch.

Dad, no doubt standing shyly with a Mexican general or two, wiggled an eyebrow at her. He had an uncanny knack for drawing women to him. It was a mystery I pondered with a certain awe: Papa was a lady-killer. (He liked that phrase. When he read, in *Playboy*, the term "swordsman," he was pixilated beyond words. Here was an English phrase at once naughty and British enough to make him think of James Bond, the gold standard of manhood in my house.) And he must have been gleaming that night. He held his cigarette just so. He blushed a bit and grinned sideways. His uniform would have been spotless and creased sharp as if he'd been planning to slice apples with it. His shoes would have been black mirrors. He still had his teeth then. His smile was a bright fire burning under a neat mustache.

Papa had it goin' on: All that and a bag of chips.

Mom, on the other side of the dance floor, was Da Bomb.

She was looking so good that an Argentine actor— unbelievable enough, an Argentine who "twirled his whiskers"—decided that Phyl was the girl for him. He began his pursuit in the single-minded way that foreign men have. Smiling, offering insincere confessions of love, pawing, pinching. Mom went from room to room with Señor Lothario close behind. He wouldn't leave her alone. She thought she'd made an escape by slipping out to the garden, only to find herself cornered. To hear her tell it, the Argentine closed in on her like Dracula. But suddenly, Alberto Urrea burst through the door and said something like, "Halt, you blackguard!" (Of course, this was in Spanish, so my mother never knew what, exactly, was said.)

The actor's fame didn't faze my father one bit. After all, he lived in the palace with the most famous men in Mexico;

the president was one of the most famous men in all of Latin America. Movie stars came through Mexico City all the time. Dad swore he saw Rita Hayworth take off her panties and throw them into a bullring when a matador caught her fancy. He was from the same village as Mexico's king of the popular song, Pedro Infante. He was good friends with the great ballad writer Agustín Lara—he even had a record by Lara in which Lara says at the beginning of the song, "This is for my blond friend, Beto Urrea." My father could have people killed with a word. What did he care about Argentine actors?

Al was nothing if not bold. I once watched him face a Chicano gangbanger by himself. The gangster had a gun, cocked. And my father gave him such a ferocious scolding that the thug actually put away the gun and ran.

Besides, she was an American woman.

"You've got to grab your balls," he once said, "and just jump."

So he defended her honor. He stood between her and her pursuer and spoke passionately enough to drive the lust-maddened cad away. He turned and took her arm and led her back to the ball. No doubt they danced. Knowing my dad, there was a smooch before the night was over.

Finally, Phyllis had found her hero.

III

How is this for a name: Aethelberht Urias of the Visigoths. It doesn't sound too Mexican, whatever *Mexican* is.

Aethelberht Urias begat Hlutwig Aethelberht Urias of the Visigoths. From Old German, Hlutwig means "famous warrior." Note to the Nazis: mine is a truly Aryan name. Hlutwig—Ludwig—Louis—Luis. Me.

If you trace the Urrea bloodline back far enough, you find that our Aryan looks are attributed to the Visigoths, when they entered Spain and generously dispersed gallons of genetic material in every burning village. And one of the Visigoth warriors who blitzed our part of Spain, siring many blond ancestors of mine, was Urias. Urias—Uria—Urria—Urrea.

It confuses me too, Homes. Here I am, a Luis Alberto, a *greaser*, and I still could have been enrolled in the SS. Did I tell you about the border patrol truck idling between my ribs?

My cousin is Apache. My other cousin is Mayo. My second cousin is black. My niece is German. One branch of the Urreas is Chinese. Other Urreas claim to be Basques. One great-grandmother was Tarascan. As I mentioned above, my paternal grandmother was a Murray—Irish. My cousins are Hubbards. Somebody tell me, please, what a Mexican is.

Mexico—the true melting pot.

We called Dad "Papa." All of us—his kids from his first marriage, my cousins, my mother, and me.

He came out of a small yet famous mining town in the south of Sinaloa. It was called Rosario, and it slumbered on the banks of the Baluarte River, beneath the strange profile of a mountain called El Yauco. My uncle always swore there was a town nearby called Palo Cagado, which means, I'm afraid, "shit on a stick."

Students of magic realism in graduate school today need only to live in a small Mexican town for a few weeks. They will soon see that this mad literary genre is based on truth. My father's memories were full of ghosts, natural catastrophes, demons, miracles, weird sex, weirder pranks, floods, appalling deaths, flying saucers, Indian spirits, and tall tales. Rosario had, for example, a self-proclaimed Practical Joke King of All Mexico. This man—Pancho Mena—terrorized the town for decades with ever more elaborate stunts. His masterpiece was a hog's head barrel suspended over the town square on a web work of ropes. In the barrel, several hundred pounds of feces collected from his outhouse. Inside the feces, a charge of dynamite with a time fuse.

My father was present when the bomb exploded. It had been timed to blow right at 7:00 A.M., when everyone who was on the way to market would have been in the square and stopped to gawk at the levitating barrel. My father was behind an adult when the barrel blew, but he remembers peeking around the man's side and being hit in the face, as if by a noxious cream pie.

Mena never saw this *tour de force,* since he had wisely boarded the dawn train for the north, never to return.

One summer, when I was living in Rosario, spending many idle boyhood hours hunting iguanas and snapping turtles, eating mangos fresh off the tree, I spent some time with my father's first girlfriend. She was famous in family lore as his lost love. She didn't call him "Papa"; she called him "Beto."

One day, she showed me a mountain with a cleft in it. She—like many Sinaloans, not at all afraid of crude speech—informed me it was known as "La Pucha," The Pussy. I stared at it, thinking, *So that's what they look like!* Inside La Pucha's caves, supposedly there was a rope that dangled out of a sheer rock wall. This was because the Spanish monks from Rosario had hidden their vast treasure of gold bars in the cave, then either died of mysterious afflictions, committed suicide, or were murdered. Their ghastly spirits still wandered the cave, often leading explorers to the gold—*but the explorers never found the gold again when they went back to collect it.* One expedition reasoned that a rope, played out behind them, would give them an easy egress from the treasure chamber. When they didn't return, rescuers followed them *and found the rope sticking out of a blank rock wall!* The other side of La Pucha was round—it featured two wooded hills meeting in a deep vertical crack. "Guess what we call this side," she said.

My father, fully steeped in Rosario's occult atmosphere, swore that the angry spirit of an Indian warrior pursued him through time. He had stolen several Aztec figurines when he was working for the president. (I have one of them still—it's a thick bead covered in small designs.) And the warrior wanted them back.

My father dreaded this spirit. It rapped on his bedroom furniture and woke him several times a night. It appeared to him in dreams. It shook him awake.

One night, he came for me well after midnight. He whispered, "Come in my room." I followed him down the hall and into his bedroom. "Touch the bed," he said. I put my hand on it. The bed was vibrating, jumping up and down as if alive. "I told you," Papa said, "that he was after me."

He was my hero and my greatest source of terror.

He was brilliant and kindhearted, and at times painfully funny. His wit was such that you couldn't tell if he was putting you on or not. When I was little, for example, he would insist that cows were horses, and horses, cows. With a perfectly straight face, he would argue the point with me until I was exasperated. He never relented. On another occasion, he brought home Mexican translations of *The Iliad* and *The Odyssey*. He claimed it was time for me to study them "in their original Spanish."

He was always a great storyteller.

On car trips, he delighted in constructing a Paul Bunyanesque alternate history of my grandfather's exploits. The Painted Desert was painted by my grandfather, for example. The bubbling "paint pots" of Yellowstone were heated by my grandfather. The Grand Canyon was excavated by my grandfather sometime around 1936—he carried the dirt and rocks out in buckets, and he used the mounds to build the Sierras.

He delighted in the foolishness of others. One of his favorite jokes (he was a walking library of off-color jokes) was about a Mexican sleeping in the shade behind a donkey. An American came by and asked him, "What time is it?" The Mexican reached up and lifted the donkey's testicles, looking under them. "It's noon," he said. Astounded, the American said, "Could you check again?" The Mexican reached up, took the donkey's testicles in hand, lifted, and peeked again. "Twelve-oh-one," he said. The American thought this was sheer magic, an ancient Mexican ritual. He rushed to get his wife. When they got back to the Mexican, the man said, "Excuse me, but could you tell my wife what time it is?" The Mexican repeated the lifting ritual and said, "Five minutes after twelve." Overcome with awe, the American fell to his knees and said, "Please, you must teach me this occult mystery! How do you do it?" The Mexican looked up at him, then gestured for the American to join him on the ground. "You see," he said, "I reach up here and lift the donkey's balls. Then I can look under his belly at the clock tower across the street. It's twelve-ten."

Americans often got the worst of my father's jokes.

"Oh Papa!" Mom would say when he told one of his stories. They slept apart, in separate bedrooms. They sat sometimes in the living room, chatting, smoking. And sometimes they towered far above me, laughing, their heads lost in blue-white clouds of smoke. Sometimes, they'd even start to reach for each other, almost embrace. But they'd stop. Look away. Leave the room. Mom would go to the kitchen. Papa would go bowling, or put on a record album with the turntable set at 45 rpms. The squeaky, sped-up voices of Vaughn Monroe or Pedro Infante would knock me to the floor, laughing.

These were the best moments.

But Papa was also consumed by rage. A burning, purple rage. Nobody knew what caused it, and nobody could predict what would set it off. Sometimes he would just explode—seem to open his chest and let a roar escape that shook the windows. At other times, he would turn cold, harsh, mechanical in his anger. This was more frightening than his eruptions.

And always, the stories. He never stopped telling stories. When the rage was upon him, he would betray my mother by telling his first wife that she staggered around the house swilling whiskey from a bottle of Jack Daniels, so drunk she couldn't make the beds. In our home, however, he would betray his first wife by telling my mother that she picked lice out of her hair, cracking them on her dirty thumbnails, or flicking them away into a corner, there to join the other vermin.

He had a favorite dog, Palito. Palito lived at my grandmother's house in Tijuana. My father adored this old dog—saved Fritos for him, loved for him to sit on his feet as he watched television. Still, one day, for no apparent reason, he drop-kicked Palito down a flight of stairs and walked away, unflustered. Later, in San Diego, neighbors were appalled to see him kicking our new dog down the street, kicking him as they ran, until they were out of sight. The dog screaming all the way.

The Machine appeared when I was to learn anything that a macho man should know how to do. Riding a bike, for example. He said to me one day when I was in first grade,

"Do you want to learn to ride a bike like a real man? Get rid of these." He gestured at the training wheels, which he hated. He had called me "Pussy" once, when I'd rattled past.

Of course I wanted to please him. He was Papa! So I said yes, and he immediately broke out a tool and undid the training wheels. Balancing me on the bike seat, in the middle of the street, with cars rushing by beside us, he said, "Ready?"

"Yeah!" I cried.

And we started to run. I felt like I was flying, with Papa's strong hands holding me upright. Until he let go.

I flew down the street. Not very far. It couldn't have been far at all. And I tumbled, sliding on the blacktop, crashing into the curb. Cars honked. I started to cry, but I realized it was a mistake. "Get up," he said. I stopped crying right away. We did it again. I was a little bloodied after the second crack-up. "Again," he said. And, "Otra vez."

It may not have been tender, but I learned to ride the bike. It only took about five crashes to get it. I suddenly knew that either I'd learn to ride it, or he'd keep at it until I was knocked out or the bike broken. It didn't matter which—a lesson, some sort of lesson, would have been learned. I am still guessing about his lessons. I suspect they had something to do with that peculiar and sometimes lamentable state called "manhood." Whatever that is.

He was ashamed that I was afraid of the waves at the beach. He enlisted the aid of another man, and they took me to the ocean and carried me into the water. I begged them not to do it. They laughed. The harder I fought, the more they laughed. They had me by the hands and feet, and they swung me back and forth, counting, "One! Two! Three!" and throwing me into the oncoming waves. The water drove me under, sand up my nose.

When I crawled out on the beach, they'd be there, waiting. Laughing. I would begin to beg again, crying; I even ran, but I couldn't outrun them. And he'd always tell me I should learn to stop crying. Maybe if I had refused to beg for mercy, they would have let me go.

Because I cried easily, he always volunteered to take me to the dentist. It would be better with Papa there was the line my mother bought. And Tijuana would be a better place for dental work because it was cheaper. We were poor. It made sense to Phyl.

The dentist was a man from Sinaloa, and he apparently had the same ethic of masculinity as my father. They agreed to work on my teeth without an anesthetic, with my father in the room. The drill wailed in my mouth, the pain forever equated in my mind with the smell of my smoking teeth. The dentist's breath. And my father staring over his shoulder. "Be a *man*, God damn it," my father said.

When I cried, they both yelled at me, using the word that, in their language, translated as "asshole."

"He wasn't always bitter," Papa's first wife told me. "He was sweet. He was sweet and innocent. He never cursed, never misbehaved. Something happened to him."

He was tight-lipped about what happened. I caught

glimpses of his story, but often from others, witnesses or those who heard from a friend of a friend. My father was the superstar of his own life. They talk about "Beto" still—about his jokes, his music (he played piano and organ), his adventures, his bowling, his women. If you had a wife, and my father entered your house, chances were he'd have made some sort of significant contact with her that would leave her touched and intrigued. Often, women fell in love with him at their first meeting. And my father would find a way to come back to see them. He could wait ten years to collect on their infatuations.

I never knew the legendary dapper Mexican officer. The Papa I knew best worked all night in bowling alleys. My hero, dusting bowling shoes with Quinsana foot powder and renting them to winos. Or waxing the lanes with a long-handled dust mop. Or sitting in the deafening roar of the walkways behind the big Brunswick pin-tending machines. I can see him there now, under the sole lightbulb, bent over a *Playboy,* smoking his Pall Malls. He also hid nudist magazines back there. I was enthralled by the absurd photographs of middle-aged volleyball players, caught in midair, breasts and privates flapping. He liked this stuff. He wanted me to know all about it.

I still remember a book he gave me. It was called *Diary of a Dirty Old Man.* It was about masturbating in every imaginable situation. Perhaps one reason he was so interested in printed, two-dimensional sex was because Mom would have none of it. Sex seemed to scare her almost as much as her worst terror, snakes. I could make her shudder just by saying "rattlesnake." If I said "python," she would actually cry out and leave the room.

"Sex" wasn't as bad as snakes. She delighted in James Bond's exploits with the "Bond girls." She just didn't want me to ever come near the evil deed. And the idea of sex with Papa . . . well.

One day, I got home from school to find her in a fury. She had a way of going wild—her hair would be in disarray and she would have a crazy gleam in her eye. She'd purse her lips, as though she were about to whistle. There was no reasoning with her in those moments.

She dragged me into his room and tore the mattress off the bed. *Oh-oh*, I thought. I couldn't believe she'd found his stash of "naughty" magazines. What was she doing lifting his mattress? He made his own bed—we were not often welcome in his room.

My mother ranted and raved, waving the magazines in front of my face. They were all low-rent nudie rags, third raters like *Pix* and *Adam* and *Knight*. All I remember her saying is the phrase, "I can understand *Playboy*, but not this FILTH!" I kept hearing that word: filth. She dragged me into the back yard, where she had a bonfire going. She tore the books and magazines apart—including the *Diary*—and threw them into the fire. She seemed insane with rage. Yelling in my face, as if I had written the things, as if the pictures were all my idea. She emptied his room of any trace of nude women, but when he came home, he didn't mention a thing. Neither did she. We all kept quiet, and there was never any mention of it again.

What happened to him? There were rumors that he suffered a serious head injury while deep in the silver mines of Rosario; others tell me this didn't happen at all. Once, he told me he'd seen a terrible accident in the mines. "I had to hold a man down when I was fourteen," he told me. "They sawed his leg off."

Rumors that his first lost love enraged him at a party by dancing with another, and my father, drunk and insane with jealousy, stole his first wife and rode away with her on a horse. Or not. Whatever happened, they were married. They had six children—one died at birth. Then he fell in love with his cousin, and the marriage ended.

He told me that the president of Mexico kept a black DC-3 airplane in a secret hangar in Mexico City. When political enemies of the PRI party were caught, the plane flew them out to the Pacific. It returned empty. He said he sometimes flew DC-3's. Was he on these flights? He never said.

Finally, what brought him to the border? Survivors say he came north to try to reconnect with that cousin. She is portrayed as a dragon lady who used my father and then cast him off. When he realized that he had been played for a fool, he married my mother on the rebound. That's their story.

His story was considerably different. He told me that after years of service to the president, he had accrued a great deal of trust and influence in the Mexican government. One day, the president of Mexico called him in to a private meeting. Papa would never tell me what was said. It still upset him. The only things he ever told me, and he said them many times over the years, were that they asked him to do something he could not do, and that they had paid him $2,000 in American money. This was quite a lot of money in Mexico City in 1951.

Relatives who heard this tale didn't believe me. Then, when he died, I was put in charge of sifting through his things. In a shoebox, mixed in with his papers and old government documents, was an uncashed check. It was made out to Alberto Urrea Murray. It was for $2,000. It was signed by the president of Mexico.

Nothing broke my father. Except for the U.S. He couldn't find his footing here. He couldn't rise again, and he knew it. He tried many jobs—busboy, cannery worker, bakery truck driver. I often think he settled on bowling alleys because he was the most erudite man there, even if he was a greaser. Al was the smart one. Al was the one who read. Al was the lover who swept Norma and all the other burger-bar waitresses off their feet with sweet Spanish, love songs, and his looks.

Whenever I think of the bowling alley, I hear Patsy Cline echoing over the lanes. "Crazy" and "I Fall to Pieces" and "Walkin' after Midnight" were the big hits in the Rip Van Winkle Lounge. The old drunks slumped in there among red vinyl booths and blue lights, smoking and staring out of the darkened windows at Papa, manning the main desk like a captain again. And Norma tipping up on her toes to steal a quick kiss, her peach waitress uniform skirt hiking up to reveal the tops of her white stockings, her tender thighs, her petticoat's hem. Maybe it wasn't the drunks. Maybe it was me, sipping a chocolate malt.

What happened? I don't think even he knew. I can tell you what happened to them, what caused the wrong turn. It was Tijuana. It was San Diego. My mother went from aristocratic surroundings to a dirt street in Tijuana, where the Mexicans didn't want her and subjected her to mental cruelties like taking a hammer to her jewelry and cutting her clothes up with shears. And my father went from being a superstar to just another beaner, doing it all legally—green-carded and registered—but still unable to touch the American Dream. Scrubbing the urinals used by white men who were far below him in every way.

Betrayed by life, by the border, by each other, my parents clung to lives they hated. It seems heroic now, looking back.

They managed to carry on when every dream they'd ever had was dashed and scattered.

They even tried to be a family when every possible definition of that word was lost to them.

They tried to be parents when they'd never even had the chance to be children.

He often told people, "Luis is not my son! He is my best friend!"

Whenever he did something, he'd touch me on the head first, for good luck.

He bought me every book and every record I wanted, even sitting through Jimi Hendrix's "Star-Spangled Banner" and saying, "Those are rockets!" as the guitar screamed.

When he met my first steady girlfriend, and I kissed her in front of him, he said, "Don't count your money in front of a pauper."

When he made chili, he went for the world record heart-stopping atomic recipe: four pork chops, two large cans of Dennison's chili, refried beans, red onions, chiles, a pound of monterey jack cheese, and a pan of Spanish rice.

He thought pancakes were exotic, and buttermilk or blue-berry pancakes drove him mad with lust.

Before he left us, he would sit for hours playing his organ. Clad in blue pajamas, chain smoking, drinking cup after cup of black coffee, he'd play. Over and over, he'd play one song, trying to get it perfect. He'd go into a kind of trance, staring at the wall, or sitting with his head thrown back, eyes closed, smiling vaguely, and oom-pa-pa-ing through "Red Roses for a Blue Lady." He was dreaming, he said, of being the lounge organist in the Rip Van Winkle Room, a glass snifter full of dollar bills, and blonde American women leaning toward him as he played.

At night, he ground his teeth. He ground them so hard that they broke in his mouth. Sometimes he swallowed the pieces. Sometimes he spit them out in the morning. By the time I was in my early teens, every tooth in his mouth was shattered. All that was left was a row of small stumps.

I learned insomnia in our house, between Al and Phyl. She was whimpering and crying out all night. He was snoring and grinding his teeth with a loud cheeping sound. All night, cries and grinding. Not even pillows over my head could keep the noise of their horrible nights out of my ears.

IV

Here's a story about a family that comes from Tijuana and settles into the 'hood, hoping for the American Dream. It's a small picture of a few moves in the chess game of disaster. The family game starting to fall apart from the buried rage and broken souls. I'm not saying it's our story. I'm not saying it isn't. It might be yours.

They lived at 3935 National Avenue.

When she was feeling well, Mother fed the birds on their narrow strip of lawn. She tore chunks from three or four slices of bread, and she and the boy tossed them out in the middle of the grass. Then they watched through the living room window, hiding behind the edge of the venetian blinds, as sparrows, pigeons, and the occasional mockingbird descended to squabble over the food. The boy thought the blinds came from Venus.

Their apartment was in the last building of the development, and the pavement of National Avenue didn't extend to the alley that ran behind their kitchen door. They lived in the lower back corner, in a two-bedroom apartment with a small kitchen/dining alcove and a living room. The boy shared one bedroom with his mother. His father slept in the other room, alone. Outside, there were the kinds of bushes that passed for greenery in Southern California. A dark-leaved hibiscus covered the opening beneath the concrete stairs to the second-story apartments. The boy had his cave there behind the bush. Sometimes, after he'd watched a Hercules movie with his father, he'd climb the outside of the stairway and leap onto the lawn, swinging a plastic sword.

Drunken men sometimes slept on the lawn, dark-skinned skinny men, lying comatose in the creeping sun after some ghetto dance party. On those days, the birds did not come. And the boy watched the men from his window, watched their bony chests rise and fall, watched the stain of urine spread sometimes, watched their fingers curl and their feet twitch as they dreamed. The soles of their feet were yellow, cracked. His mother called them terrible names, and they thought worse things about her but dared not say them.

On the Fourth of July, Dad was usually out with friends, and Mom was too afraid of the neighborhood to walk the mile and a half to the public park for the fireworks. So she'd make popcorn, and she and the boy would climb to the landing halfway up. From there, they could see the colored flashes lighting the sky behind a stand of trees. It looked like lightning inside a cloud, only it was red, violet, yellow, blue. Sometimes, slim puffs of smoke angled out from the tree crowns, and they turned dark before the reflected glow of the explosions. Every once in a while, a bit of the actual fireworks would rise high enough to clear the treetops. It was shocking—like a chunk of the sky catching fire and throwing an ember. Years later, those balmy nights remained precious to him. His mother in her dresses, her dark hair pulled back by a pale headband, flickering in silhouette against the colored sky. She sat primly, knees together, hands in lap, looking over her shoulder. As he stared up at her so lost in the spectacle, she sometimes seemed one hundred feet tall, a sorrowful monument thrown up against the dark.

Burr clover grew all over the lawn. It had tiny yellow flowers, and its tightly rolled burrs could be peeled open if you were patient and careful. You could unroll them, and minuscule yellow-green seeds revealed themselves. The boy often harvested the seeds and put them in his plastic army helmet. Then he'd go to other parts of the lawn and scatter them, trying to make something grow.

There was sourweed in the shade around the base of the biggest bushes. Pill bugs and snails could always be found there, and sometimes beetles. The occasional earwig frightened him—he thought the pincers on their tails meant they were baby scorpions. The pill bugs looked like Volkswagens. He suspected they might be baby armadillos. He picked sourweed stalks and chewed them, his lips puckering at the bitter taste. The black kids said the taste was from dog pee, but he didn't believe them. He was in third grade.

Across the lawn, Their apartments began. *They*.

They had some fuchsias and poinsettias left over from the days of white families, but the lawn was already going yellow between the buildings. The landlords sold out to welfare leases, then promptly stopped attending to their buildings. The boy didn't venture into the further reaches of the complex, but he knew there was a mattress moldering on the lawn at 3930, a broken television set on the walkway at 3929, and a wall coming down at 3925. His father offered reports of each new development when he got home from work.

"There's a God-damned television out there," he'd say. "The first thing they buy is a television."

"Or a Cadillac," Mom said.

"Then they don't know how to take care of them," Dad said.

Mom had decided to block off the stairs. She used potted geraniums—three pots per step, nine in all, because "those people will just walk up to your door and stare in at you. Looking for something to steal."

One day, while they were out, one of Their fathers came up on the porch and broke every pot. The boy's family came home to dirt and fragments of brightly painted clay scattered all over the steps. The little geranium twigs lay murdered in the dirt. They reminded him of broken umbrellas. He stood and watched Mom and Dad clean the mess, afraid less of the violence than of his parents' response to it.

The boy didn't know what Mom did in there when she sent him out to play. The apartment was usually dark—they didn't like the blinds open to let in too much sun. His father was off driving a bread truck.

He'd started out as a waiter. Then he'd worked at Chicken of the Sea canning tuna. He was restless. Nothing suited

him. He was small, compact. Supercharged. The boy
thought his father's hands had the thickest, strongest fingers
in the world.

Now, he was driving a 1961 Chevy panel truck, leased
out from Helm's Bakery. It was two-tone—pale yellow with
black fenders—and in back there were large wooden draw-
ers full of doughnuts, cookies, pies, cakes. The area directly
behind the driver's seat had racks of bread and bins of rolls.
On the roof of the cab was a little train whistle, and the
driver could pull a chain and the truck would go *woo-woo.*

In spite of his nasty racial views, he couldn't bear to see
the poor mothers on his route. Black mothers. He extended
so much credit to them that he was going out of business.
He drove longer hours, longer miles, and earned less by a
dollar or two a day. He was driving himself to bankruptcy.
In the afternoons when Mom came home from work, she'd
send the boy outdoors. Then she'd go inside and shut the
door and stay shut in until six o'clock, when Dad came home.

And the boy would pull himself slowly out of the dusk,
into the painful light of the kitchen.

He liked the back of the apartment more than the front.
In the front, there was the cave under the stairs. But the
back offered poisonous plants. When he was sure Mom
wasn't looking, he broke open poinsettia stalks and watched
the milk seep out. Everyone said it would kill you. It fasci-
nated him. It smelled bland, like the smell in all the other
plants when you crumpled their leaves. It also smelled a
little like the black soil beneath the rocks at the edge of the

alley. He'd almost let the milk touch his fingers before he pulled them away. Death, right in his hand. He thought it might be like falling asleep.

Then, of course, there was the alley. He delighted in the alley—its wide dirt and rock surface was a wilderness to him, a desert in the middle of the neighborhood. When it rained, he saw swamps, dark King Kong rivers teeming with monsters: he sank his plastic dinosaurs in up to their haunches.

The alley sloped downhill and turned left, behind the row of detached garages. At the far end of the garages was a small washroom with two washing machines and two dryers. Dad had the first garage. When he came home from work, the boy raced to the door and pulled it open. Dad drove in and set the hand brake. He and the boy checked the daddy longlegs that hung upside down beneath the dashboard in its paltry web.

"He's my buddy," Dad said. "My pet."

The boy always liked it when Dad was in his gooder mood. Sometimes Dad had his cranky mood, and the whole house turned dark gray inside and nobody spoke too loud. The gooder mood was full of jokes and Bert Kaempfert records. When Mom was in her cranky mood, they would crash together and everything would be broken, lights out, Dad gone, Mom in bed howling boo-hoos, just like in fairy tales. Boo-hoo!

They walked to the rear of the truck.

"Let's check the inventory," Dad said.

Yep, definitely feeling gooder today.

He opened the big door at the back and pulled open the top drawer. The indelible odor of bakeries escaped: chocolate, cinnamon, dough. In their wax-paper-lined compartments, doughnuts stood on end, tightly packed.

"I don't know . . ." Dad said. "It seems to me the best doughnut ever made is the glazed."

"No, Dad," the boy said. "It's a chocolate-coated."

"What!"

"Really." He pointed at the row of chocolate-coated cake doughnuts, pushed together like the coils of some delicious snake. "The best."

Dad reached in and plucked a huge glazed one out with a square of wax paper.

"But look at this," he said. He turned it like some fine piece of jewelry.

"Chocolate," the boy said.

Dad took out a chocolate doughnut with the other hand.

"No comparison," he said.

"Cho-co-late, Dad," the boy said.

Dad shook his head sadly.

"Well," he sighed. "I suppose we're going to have to taste them." He took a bite of the glazed. "Mf," he said.

The boy grabbed his doughnut from his father and took a bite. The hard chocolate cracked, and the golden fried cake dough broke all over his tongue.

They sat on the back bumper eating their doughnuts, the boy's legs swinging.

"Mine's better," he said.

They got done, slammed the truck door shut, pulled down the garage door, and headed up the alley. It was turning dark. His father smelled of sweat and cigarette smoke. He poked the boy in the gut with one finger and said, "Butter-ball."

He did not smile.

The boy laughed really loud.

"Wipe your mouth," Dad said. "And don't tell your mother I gave you a doughnut."

The boy's lips, in the gloom, looked like they were covered in blood.

She was in the kitchen heating TV dinners. Dad always ate turkey with gravy. Mom and the boy ate "fried" chicken, with apple cobbler in one triangular compartment. She was cutting lettuce in small pieces for a salad.

Dad put his lunch bucket on the aluminum table and said, "Hi." She kept her back to him. The boy shook a little turtle food into the turtle tank. The yellow-eyed turtle inside was stretched out on the plastic ramp beneath the palm tree. "Don't feed him too much," Dad said. "You'll make him fat."

He rummaged in the fridge.

"Would you like some sherry?" he said, taking a bottle out.

"Oh, a little Thunderbird might be nice," she said.

He put one bottle back, took out another. He filled two small glasses.

"Can I have a sip?" the boy said.

"No," Mom said.

Dad said, "Just a little sip." He winked.

"You want it here or out there?" he said to Mom.

"I'll join you," she said.

"Fine," he said.

She glanced at him.

"Hm," she said.

Dad took a small soup bowl and emptied a bag of Fritos into it. Then he shook a bunch of cashews into the bowl on top of the Fritos.

"I'll carry it," the boy said.

They went into the other room, Dad carrying the glasses, the boy carrying the bowl. They set it all down on a small TV tray table beside Dad's favorite white chair. He sat and said, "Ah."

He shook the last Pall Mall out of the pack on the tray.

"Turn on the TV," he said. "Channel eight. Cronkite."

The boy switched on the television.

Dad lit his cigarette.

There was a small crash in the kitchen.

"*Shit*," Mom muttered.

"That's nice," said Dad. "Isn't that nice, Son, to talk like that?"

Thinking he was in on a joke, the boy said, "Yeah, Mom. Real nice!"

He and Dad giggled.

Dad gave him a small sip of Thunderbird.

Mom came in and sat in her chair, placed exactly three feet from Dad's. Its feet had made four precise little holes in the carpet. She picked up one Frito with her nails and bit it. Then she sipped her drink. She lit a cigarette.

"Aren't we hilarious?" she said.

Cronkite's brow was furrowed as he reported on Negro

unrest and strange developments in Cuba. "President Kennedy," he was saying.

"Rub my feet," Dad said.

The boy sat between his feet and began to unlace Dad's work shoes. They had thick, rippled rubber soles.

"Must you do that before supper?" said Mom.

"He can wash his hands," said Dad.

He worked the shoes off. Dad always wore black socks. He had about twelve pairs of identical black socks. He was never without a match in his sock drawer. Still, he carefully rolled each pair together and kept them neat. When he ended up with an extra sock, he threw it away. The boy rolled his socks down, over Dad's high arches, and off. Dad's feet were white as grubs. His toes were square and stubby. The boy put the socks inside the shoes.

"Get between my toes," Dad said.

The boy massaged Dad's feet, starting on the ball and moving up to the toes then back to the heel. He reached between Dad's toes and peeled out the tattered little flags of skin blistered up by athlete's foot. First the right foot, then the left, pushing in between Dad's toes with his fingertips.

He could tell it felt good.

When things felt good to Dad, he made a little sucking gasp: *Sst-unh. Sst-unh.*

Dad waited till the boy was absorbed by his work, then he snapped his ear. He liked to flick it with one nail when he wasn't expecting it, make the kid jump. Old Jug Ear.

"Ow!" the boy said.

Dad laughed, prodded the boy away with his foot.

"Don't talk back to me," he said.

"Wash your hands," Mom said.

As he ran the water over his hands, he could hear them in there sniping at each other. When he turned the water off, it ended. Like magic.

Dinner was served when he came out. Mom and Dad had their small trays of food set on their TV tables, with saucers of salad. Their glasses full of amber liquid jittered as they cut their food.

His supper was set out on the kitchen table. His napkin was folded in a neat triangle. He ate alone.

Whenever he complained, he was told, "You will learn to eat like a decent human being, at a fully set table."

Mom with her weird little rules.

He stared at the turtle. It stared at him. The batter on the chicken was soggy. It stuck to his mouth. He avoided the compartment with the gray peas and perfectly cubed cooked carrots.

"Drink your milk," Mom said.

"I will."

"Want some bread?" said Dad.

"Would you *like* some bread?" Mom corrected.

"Jesus Christ," muttered Dad.

He could hear him gobbling his food. Dad breathed through his nose as he ate. He sounded like an engine. He ate like a starving dog. Sometimes the way Dad ate scared him.

"Yeah."

"Manners," Mom said. "We won't have our boy speaking like white trash."

"Yes," the boy said. "Please."

Mom came into the kitchen and buttered two slices of bread. She cut the bread diagonally and set it on a saucer, then placed the saucer on the table. She ruffled his hair.

"How's supper, Honey?"

"Fine."

She patted his head.

"That's good." Then, suddenly overcome with emotion, she grabbed him in a desperate hug. Her forearm dug into his throat and choked him.

"My eensie-teensie-weensie baby boy," she said.

She kissed him. He ducked his head away from her. The turtle slid off its ramp and plopped into the water.

"A little more Thunderbird?" Mom called out.

"Don't you think you've had enough?" Dad said.

"Let's not be ridiculous," Mom said. "I've only had one glass. The way you carry on, a person would think you're an old woman!"

The boy turned in his chair and looked at Dad.

Dad was staring at the television, his face red. His jaw muscle worked furiously in his cheek. He took a drag on his cigarette and glanced at his son. He let smoke leak out of his mouth.

"*Eensie-teensie,*" Dad said.

Back to supper. The cobbler was gooey and sweet. He chewed it carefully, in little tiny bites to make it last. The baked cinnamon apple chunks burst between his molars.

Mom poured herself another little glass.

"Papa's going *bowling* tonight," she said brightly. "Doesn't that sound like fun?" She walked out of the kitchen. "I can't imagine a more fascinating evening! So athletic!"

"Have another drink," Dad said. "Show us how sophisticated you are."

"Oh, *Papa!* You have put me in my place."

"Bitch, bitch, bitch," Dad muttered.

On TV the mystery guest was signing his name on a card. The audience applauded wildly.

"Can I come out?" the boy said.

Dad stubbed out his cigarette butt.

"Bring me a new pack when you come," he said.

The boy rummaged under the sink, broke open a red carton, and peeled the cellophane off the new pack. He came out and sat between Dad's legs again. Dad tapped the pack against his knuckle, shaking one cigarette loose.

Dad must have gotten the idea right then—he got those ideas all the time. Real good ones. Creative. He liked to play little pranks, scare his *hijo* a little, toughen him up. Like, when they were up high, on a cliff above the ocean or on a high bridge, Dad liked to grab him and start to throw him off, yanking him back at the last second. The boy fell for it every time. Dad would go "Whoo!" when he did it. The boy would scream.

Pendejo.

Dad was about to strike the match to light his fresh cigarette. He was looking at the back of the boy's head, the flatness of it and the cowlick. The boy's ears drove Dad nuts. Dad put the match on the sandpaper strip, ready to strike it; it had to be perfect for the gag.

"Hey," he said.

"Huh?" said the boy, still staring at the TV.

"Hey. Look."

The boy turned around.

Dad struck the match and thrust it at his face. Mom shouted. Dad said: "Whoo!" The boy, startled, opened his mouth in a gasp. Dad had already started to laugh. The match went between the boy's lips as the sulfur ignited. The match head burst into flame, searing the corner of his mouth. His lips sealed around the flame and stuck together. Dad's eyes widened. The boy clawed at his face, screamed, ran out of the room. Mom knocked over her chair as she ran after him.

"What'd I do?" Dad was shouting.

He sat there in his white chair, waving his cigarette.

"It was a joke, God damn it! What do you think, I did it on purpose?"

He could hear them in the bathroom, making a fuss.

"Stop crying, you baby!"

He ate some Fritos.

"It was a God-damned joke!"

V

"Joke" is a Latin word. "God" is Old English. "Damn" is Latin. "Mother" is Old English, as is "Father," as is "Son."

"Family" is Latin.

"Forgive" is English.

William Carlos Williams, that most American of poets, was half Puerto Rican. "Carlos" wasn't just a New England WASP affectation. He was a Latino, just like me. He was a half-breed, just like me. He was an American. And he said:

"Of mixed ancestry, I felt from earliest childhood that America was the only home I could ever possibly call my own. I felt that it was expressedly founded for me, personally, and that it must be my first business in life to possess it."

America is home. It's the only home I have. Both Americas. All three Americas, from the Arctic circle to Tierra del Fuego.

I'm not old enough to write my memoir. Yet I'd feel as if I'd cheated if I didn't try to share some observations. So many of us live in a nightmare of silence. We are sons and daughters of a middle region, nobody's children, marching under a starless flag. Some of us wave a black flag of anarchy, and others a red flag of revolution. But most of us are waving a white flag of surrender.

My life isn't so different from yours. My life is utterly alien compared to yours. You and I have nothing to say to each other. You and I share the same story. I am Other. I am you.

So, I've offered here a few words about my part of the journey. We're all heading the same way, after all. Whether we choose to walk together or separately, we're going toward night. I am lucky. I have the angels of words beside me. So many of us are silent.

Words are the only bread we can really share.

When I say "we," I mean every one of us, everybody, all of you reading this. Each border patrol agent and every trembling Mexican peering through a fence. Every Klansman and each NAACP office worker. Each confused mother and every disappointed dad.

For I am nobody's son.

But I am everyone's brother.

So come here to me.

Walk me home.

 Part Two

Tijuana Wonderland

When I was a boy, Tijuana was a place of magic and wonder, a place of dusty gardens laden with fruit, of pretty women, dogs, food, music. Everywhere you looked, there were secrets and astonishments. And everyone was laughing.

The crime writer Ovid Demaris had an early success with a lurid book about Tijuana called Poso del Mundo. *The Hole of the World. That pretty much sums up all our feelings about "the Calcutta of the border." Along with several other writers, I have made a certain career lately of exploring the demonic face of Tijuana. But what I never told you about the place is that it was also Wonderland—my favorite town on earth.*

I. We Have Always Lived near the Castle

My grandfather was a visionary who came north to Tijuana before I was born. His hope was to establish a commune. The members thought to bake health bread to support themselves. Along with this commune, my grandfather intended to pursue his explorations into Rosicrucianism and occult science, as well as launch a career as a poet. Nobody is quite clear about why he chose Tijuana, but then, why does anyone choose Tijuana? In the old days, when Tía Juana's whorehouse lay on the low bank of that meandering nameless river, everybody knew why. But Grandpa had the border-urge-for-no-reason, even down in Sinaloa. It's an itch we have gotten to know all too well; the rash seems to be an epidemic sweeping Latin America.

Grandfather wrote his poems on a giant scroll, rolling the pages onto the ever-thickening tube of verse. In an unexpected development, he died, and his children burned all his poems. No one seems to know why these poems had to go, but go they did, leaving one stubborn line that resonated in my own father's mind for decades: "Give me two wings and watch me fly."

I always suspected this line came from the day my grandfather realized that gravity did not exist. It happened on the train ride with my father, then a young boy, from Sinaloa into the interior. They were waiting for the train to pull out. My grandfather pointed out a fly hovering in the middle of the car. When the train began to move, the fly remained exactly in place. The train sped up; the fly stayed hovering over the exact spot on the floor. "Why does he not zoom backwards and hit the back wall?" my grandfather asked. "There is no gravity," he answered himself.

This lesson stayed with my father, and he passed it on to me.

The family house seemed to grow out of a hillside in Colonia Independencia. It's still there, if you know where to look, though my cousin Hugo might shoot you if you show up unannounced. Hugo has his pistols loaded with buckshot instead of slugs. One time a neighborhood drunk kept disturbing Hugo's beloved throat-eating herd of Dobermans. Hugo came out of the house and ran down the street shooting at the guy until the guy's pants were soaked in piss as he ran and begged for his life. This is the kind of joke Hugo appreciates. If you stop by, be polite.

My grandfather built the house, energized by the lack of gravity. However, some other mysterious force slowed down the construction, and the house remained unfinished. It was a two-story, but the slope of the hill made the front door actually open on the second floor; the first floor was half subterranean and hidden. Hey, no problem: the house next door had a home-built balcony that pitched and yawed most gently. The walkers upon it had the aspect of sailors on a small boat. Later, the entire house hunched its shoulders and leaned out of plumb. It was vaguely trapezoidal and somehow jolly for its angle.

Our house had a living room and a bedroom and a dining room and a kitchen on the top (first) floor. There was also to be a second bedroom, but that mysterious power stopped my grandfather from actually putting it up, so the dining room opened onto a wonderful open room that overlooked the canyons and bustling streets of Tijuana. There, drooping clotheslines waved the Urrea flag: giant old lady underpants.

I spent much time out there, shooting toy guns, watching eclipses, inspecting the arcana of panties, fooling with the ubiquitous Tijuana geraniums, and spying through windows with Hugo's telescope. Underpants in action!

Also on this sort-of room/more-or-less roof were dogs who delighted in hanging their heads over the edge and engaging passing dogs, cats, and humans in a crazed, ear-flopping, vertical volley of insults and slobber.

Next door, Ernesto James had an outhouse that would kill a warthog at twenty paces. Pigeons, perversely delighting in the stench clouds, lived in its rafters. Hugo showed no mercy for birds that smelled like cosmic turds, so he'd plink them out of the air with a BB gun he got somewhere. Ernesto James, not to be outdone, got drunk some nights and chased the moon around his yard. We could hear him shouting, "Son of a bitch! *Luna cabrona!*" and then he'd shoot at it. He had a revolver that made a dull pop like a firecracker, and we'd stay inside lest a stray moon shot drill us through the tops of our heads. As far as I know, he never did hit the moon.

Elsewhere in the house's history: the biggest ants north of the equator have been trying steadily since 1955 to undermine the house and send it into the *arroyo*. They tunnel and excavate, but some stubbornness in the foundation won't let the house collapse yet. Besides, the ants think that gravity will help, but we know better.

We watched gringo TV and Mexican TV. My heroes were Johnny Downs ("Howdy-howdy-howdy!") and Bob Dale. But I also had Juan Luis Curiel—general purpose host to every available show "*espectacular*" on channel twelve, and the Four Seasons of Tijuana—Los Moonglow. In terms of TV, I was doubly rich.

Downstairs, there were a couple of bedrooms, a toilet, and the demon. But we'll get back to the demon later.

Nobody in the *barrio* knew what to make of the castle. Oh sure, this fellow had come along and bought a small pinnacle above the foot of Rampa Independencia (the spectacularly unpaved road that tried to destroy every car making its way to the Colonia). That was suspicious enough—who would want a hill to himself? This proved outright that something was seriously wrong. At the very least, he probably thought he was better than everybody else, and nothing could make a Mexican madder.

Work began on the mystery man's dream home. People took it in stride.

But then this man on the hill revealed his intentions. He turned his cement-block house into a castle. A castle! Old folks gawked. Battlements, little archery slots along the roof line. Nobody could see if there was a drawbridge and moat or not. His towers threw their shadows upon the small gaggle of houses and beauty shops across the Rampa. These shops, by the way, were built with their front doors exactly five-and-a-half feet away from the open mouth of a storm drain that carried rain floods away from the castle. Presumably, these storm surges would come through the front door, maybe pause for a perm and a quick cuticle job, before tearing on down the hill and flooding the Cine Reforma.

Rumors flew. He was a general, a retired general, a colonel. The president. The former president. A warlock. A Mafia kingpin. A white slaver. He was kind, rich, evil, mad, a Russian, or a gringo. Then, as if sensing the consternation in the neighborhood and savoring it, the bastard painted the whole thing bright yellow!

It loomed up there, visible from a mile away. Nobody knew exactly what was afoot, but the yellow paint could mean only one thing: the colonel was laughing at us. As far as I know, nobody ever went up there and asked him what was the deal.

One sunny day, beneath this suspicious yellow insult, in a deep pit, I first discovered death.

II. Viva la Muerte

Hugo was nuts for *The Outer Limits*. He was also the newest *karateka* in the family, mastering blood-freezing karate moves in his underground kingdom—our downstairs second floor. He pounded his fists and fingertips into buckets full of gravel. "Fingers of steel," he'd warn me, going slant-eyed and holding up the deadly knife blade of his hand. "I could pull your heart out!"

The one *Outer Limits* that got under his skin was the one where David "Illya Kuryakin" McCallum got in a time machine and turned into a man from the future. His head expanded into a brain-bubble, almost exactly like the Jiffy-Pop foil container did. This future man obsessed Hugo, and he drew the bubblehead all over the walls downstairs.

I was down there checking out his drawings with his sister, my cousin Margo. Margo weighed about seven pounds—all eyelashes and eyes. She was the only girl in the world who would hold my hand. Plus she taught me feminine secrets like Dippity-Do. She smelled like soap, bubble gum, and Vicks VapoRub.

There was a small craze in Tijuana in those days. Kids were taking the little rectangular batteries out of transistor radios and licking the terminals. Yow! It wasn't exactly a shock—it was kind of like a lick of Satan's salsa.

Anyone who has spent much time in Mexico knows that appalling things regularly go into our mouths. Take, for instance, those sickening little greasy shrimps you find in filthy plastic bags. Or how about blood pudding? (We call it *relleno*, not to be confused with *chile relleno*. I once made this unfortunate error and was served a steaming platter of what looked like black whipped cream full of onion chunks. A king-sized fried blood clot. I had dark orange teeth for the rest of the day.) And, of course, we have *saladitos*, brine-soaked prunes. Yum! Eat three of them, and you need immediate triage; an IV drip is strongly recommended.

"Let's lick the battery," Hugo suggested, opening the radio.

"No," said Margo. "Luis will do it."

"Will not!" I said, quite reasonably.

"Will too," Hugo explained, jamming the battery into my mouth.

Zzing!

I got a free perm.

After my electrocution, we went up to the street. James Brown came on. We called him "Chayss Brrong." It was as close as we could get. Also popular on the Rampa were Los Hermanos Righteous. Margo knew the dances: she could squirm like an earthworm. Hugo and I managed half-hearted shuffles in the dirt.

Suddenly Margo said, "Wanna see the bear?"

"What bear?" Hugo wanted to know.

"There's a bear down the street."

"Ha!" he scoffed.

"Come on and I'll show you."

We started off straightaway, hiking down the Rampa. On our right, the bluff at the end of which stood the castle. On our left, the slope that terminated in the backyards of a bunch of little houses below. We balanced on the crumbling edge, sending dirt clods tumbling into the yards, squinting and waving the dust away when a suicidal driver rattled and clanged over the rocks in the street. I remember whole fleets of ugly '49 Chevies, Chevies all over the hill, all of them with sun visors over their windshields.

"There," said Margo, pointing down imperiously.

Twelve feet down, looking up at us, was, as promised, a bear.

"Chingado," Hugo noted.

The bear asked, "Floob?"

It was chained to a tree stump. It was raggedy and dusty and its coat hung loose on its bones. We couldn't figure out what it was doing there. It raised its paw and waved, rattled its chain.

"Told you," Margo said.

It looked like wooden furniture under a black rug. But it also looked like a bear. I hid behind Margo.

It shook its head, got up, shuffled around, sat back down.

It was wondering what we thought we were doing in its barrio, no doubt.

It said, "Fnarff."

Hugo took control of the situation.

"Big deal," he said. "You can stand around and stare at the bear all day. But *I'm* going down the storm drain."

The storm drain!

It was absolutely, unquestionably, one hundred percent verboten. But he was already sauntering farther down the hill. Margo and I looked at each other and followed.

The bear was saying: "Moob? Mooble-fooble!"

We stood at the edge of the pit, the unseen yellow castle of evil high above us.

The drain went straight down. It was perfectly square, made of rather beautiful stonework sunk in webs of cement. The bottom was, oh, a mile away. It had a floor of pale sand. Tijuana's usual rubble filled the corners: dry weeds, paper, bottles, rags.

"How do we get down?" I asked.

"Like this," said Hugo. He grabbed me and swung me over the edge and let me drop. I hit the bottom on my rump with a small yelp and looked up. He was gawking down at me, head upside down just like the second-story dogs back at the house. In fact, I thought he was barking, but he was laughing. Margo, beside him, stared down. I could see up her skirt.

"Ayiii!" *sensei* Hugo-san bellowed as he flew down upon me.

Margo carefully hung her toe over the edge like she was stepping into water, then scrabbled down the wall like a cat.

Before us, the black maw of the tunnel, angling down under the Rampa. In the distance, at least another twenty or thirty miles away, a small square nugget of light glowed.

"All right, cowards," Hugo said. "Let's go."

We forged ahead. I hung onto Margo's skirt. Margo hung onto Hugo's shirt. Hugo said stuff like: "Beware . . . of the . . . *giant* . . . hungry . . . *tarantulas!*" Margo and I had just suffered through *Rodan,* and there were these giant slugs in a flooded tunnel that ate Japanese soldiers and we just didn't think it was that funny. "Bats," Hugo said, *"that eat . . . out . . . your . . . eyeballs."*

We smelled it first.

This awful stench came at us with delicate fingers, sort of tickled at our noses in the dark.

"Who farted?" Hugo wanted to know.

But the stink got worse: it was the worst thing I'd ever smelled.

"I'm gonna barf!" I said.

"Not on me," said Margo, snatching her skirt away.

"Hey!" I said, waving my hands around trying to find her hem.

"Be quiet," said Hugo.

Then we heard it—this slurpy wet sound. I knew it! It was those Japanese tunnel worms!

"Better look," said Hugo.

He dug in his pockets. He always had contraband in his pockets: bullets, cigarettes, knives, tops. He pulled out some matches and lit one.

We gasped.

There, lying on its side and smiling broadly at us was the corpse of a pig. Its forelegs were crossed casually. Its whole body was packed full of maggots. We watched its sides ripple and undulate as the maggots ate frantically.

"Mmm-mm, bacon!" Hugo enthused.

"Gyah!" Margo said.

"Mama!" I cried.

Hugo's match went out. He lit another.

"Death," he said, suddenly fifty years old. "It's just death. Fuck it. It's got nothing to do with us. Let's go buy some ice cream."

And he led us out.

III. Chronicle of a Death Forestalled

Of course, death is as familiar to a Mexican as life: it is a constant companion. I'd already learned where life comes from. An older boy had taken me into a field and shown me little gauzy spider egg sacks in the tall grass.

"Know what that is?" he said.

"No."

"That's unborn babies!"

"It is?"

"Yeah. When your mom wants a baby, she comes out here and picks one of these and puts it up her thing. Then it grows into a baby inside her thing."

"Wow!"

I was afraid to walk in that grass—what if I squished a couple of future *camaradas*?

Now I knew what death looked like, too. Nobody could tell me where death came from, only what it was. However, we all knew what—or who—came from death.

I remember my uncle Carlos Hubbard telling me once, "Every alley in Mexico has its own ghost."

Forget the Haunted House—if you want ghosts, we got 'em here. Tijuana is the Haunted City.

We had no proof that the bear on the Rampa was a real bear and not a ghost. We discussed going down and touching it in a limited caucus, but the motion was voted down in a landslide: Margo and Luis voting no, and the karate delegate voting yes. And who knew what wraiths floated through the halls of the castle?

My Aunt Irma, Ladies' Bowling Champeen of Mexico, claimed that Grandpa's ghost could be summoned from the land of the dead. "He's my father," she told me. "He still has his responsibilities."

"Why do you call him, *Tía?*" I asked.

"For bowling, of course!"

Apparently, Grandpa swooped into whatever bowling alley Aunt Irma was dominating, and he laid his spirit hands upon her Brunswick ball and guided it to strikes. He was especially effective at cleaning up a troubling 7–10 split. He apparently made several appearances across the border at the Bowlero. I'm not sure if winning a tournament by means of ghosts is cheating or not.

The Urreas thought those ghosts were a riot.

A big party event at the Rampa was levitating tables. The adults would gather around card tables and lay their hands on them and up they'd go. Rising off the ground, everybody hooting. Also, rapping was great dead guy fun. (Not "Baby Got Back"—knocking on things.) They'd light up their ever-present Pall Malls and talk to whatever lonesome dead guy was floating around, and he'd knock on the table.

I got rather worried about the dead for a while. What if some dead woman floated into the bathroom while I was pooing? Did dead little girls watch me take baths? What if Grandpa caught me *touching my weenie?*

Personally, I found these dead folks intrusive.

I had good reason, too. Family legend has it that a ghost used to visit me in my crib. The weird thing is that I remember him.

My father used to say that he'd carry me downstairs and put me in my crib, then stand at the door and watch me. He said I used to stare up at the ceiling and laugh, reach out to somebody, watch something fly all over the room. Okay, Dad. Fine.

I do have a memory of what was in the room, though. It was a black wisp of smoke in the shape of a man. He wore a trench coat and hat. He came up from under the door, wafting out of the crack at the bottom.

Either that, or I'm remembering a Bela Lugosi movie that was on *Science Fiction Theater*.

Grandpa Urrea is not the only meddlesome ghost in the family. According to Rampa tales, he himself was intervened upon by the dead.

Things had gone badly for the visionary commune he'd planned. Apparently, baking bread was not the ticket, but they couldn't find out what the ticket was. The commune went bust. Furthermore, his dabblings in arcane Rosicrucian secrets got him into serious trouble with the Catholic church. My father always insisted that he was excommunicated, though he was probably boasting.

Grandpa's whole world was falling in around him, and one night, he paced and paced, unable to sleep. He had a pistol, some say, and he was planning to shoot himself. He walked in the garden, around and around, smoking, trying to get up the nerve to pull the trigger.

The kids were watching. They heard a woman's voice softly talking to him. They couldn't see her in the dark. He stopped at one point to light a fresh cigarette, and in the match flare, they saw a beautiful woman with long hair held up by a crimson comb.

After a time, he calmed down and came inside.

Not another word was said until many years later, after he'd died. Due to some development down in the homeland (the details are never in sharp focus in these tales), several of the brothers were called on to supervise the moving of Grandpa Urrea's mother's grave. Our great-grandmother. She had died many years before the garden incident. And— you can see this coming, can't you?—when the casket was exhumed, it fell open, and there was a skull with a crimson comb stuck in its remaining hair! The old-timers insisted that she had returned from the dead to make her son live.

I was so aware of ghosts at this point, that anything macabre seemed possible. My grandmother burned incense compulsively. When I found the little gray cones of ash, poised perfectly on bookshelves and countertops, I was terrified. I thought they were the ashes of burned-up bodies. One time I touched one and it collapsed. I hightailed it out to the yard and hid behind the pomegranate tree.

IV. Stairway to Heaven

This part sounds like a bad joke: "There were these two dogs, stuck together in the street." However, there were these two dogs, stuck together in the street. I kept watching them through the window. They were facing in opposite directions. If they'd been facing the right way, I might have gotten it. But I was having a little trouble catching the drift.

We all thought concretely. My father was having some trouble with English. "I don't get it," he'd say. "I go to the bathroom, right? And I'm supposed to *take a piss.*" He'd think a minute. "But I'm not *taking* a piss. I'm *leaving* a piss!"

This really disturbed him. He spent years trying to get to the bottom of the mystery.

"Am I taking the piss *to* the toilet?"

Sometimes we'd sit around and work on it. "If I'm taking a crap, where am I taking it?"

So, concretely speaking, the dogs were a puzzle.

I called my aunt.

I said, "Tía, somebody tied these dogs together!"

She came out from the kitchen for a look.

"Idiot!" she said.

She had a funny way of dealing with us kids. Hugo, Margo, and I were often known as "idiots" for whatever breach of reason we'd managed. Once, when I was sleeping on the couch, I was startled to hear her in the other room farting. Whoa! I'd never heard a woman fart. *Brroom!* my aunt exulted. *Frrapp!*

I almost gagged on my pillow, I was laughing so hard. Suddenly, her door banged open in the dark and she said: "You idiot! Haven't you ever heard a God-damned fart before?"

Brraptt!

Needless to say, she wasn't impressed.

"You think you're so innocent," she said. She went back into the kitchen in a huff. Apparently, I had made an appallingly offensive scene without having any idea of what I was doing.

The dogs, looking somewhat abashed by now, scooted around, backward and forward.

"Stop watching that," said my aunt. She handed me some change. "Go out and buy me a kilo of tortillas. Make yourself useful."

I took the money and headed out the door.

The Colonia was lively as ever. Aside from the push-me–pull-you dogs, scruffy gangs of kids were playing marbles in the dirt. The ice cream man pushed his little wooden wagon selling *paletas*. Another man pushing the exact same wagon was selling steaming hot ears of corn. Their magic skill really involved my brain: how did one keep his treats icy while the other kept his hot? Huge water trucks rumbled through with bad boys hanging onto the backs. Old ladies swept tides of dust off sidewalks. The mailman marched sharply from yard to yard blowing his whistle. Brilliant kites rattled in the phone lines like slaughtered pterodactyls. The hill was jumpin'.

The *tortillería* was the world's jolliest sweat lodge. The heat was always high from the massive sheet of iron kept hot by eternally burning propane burners. Six or eight women worked in there all day, sweating and yelling over the sound of a radio. You could smell the holy *maíz* heating and sending out its incense all over the street. You could smell it from two blocks away. And the sound of their palms on the corn dough was audible from at least one block distant. *Pit-pat, pit-pat, pit-pat.*

That sound lies within the heart of everyone who relied on fresh corn tortillas every day, a sound now replaced by heartless machinery that presses out tortilla analogues on conveyer belts. That's why Old Town San Diego keeps tortilla makers in restaurant windows. Something sacred is going on and it gets in the blood.

I would stand at the counter and peer up at them. Those women, with all their mysteries and their laughter. *Pit-pat, pit-pat.* Everybody was poor, but who knew? Their arms—the richest most enjoyable brown—jiggled as they worked. Their hair, deep black, wound into immense braids, lay pinned to their necks or held back by cloth. *Pit-pat.*

They ground the corn in big stone *metates,* both the corn and the stone handed down through generations from the Aztecs, still bearing Aztec names. Their hands repeated the motions of millions of hands and hundreds of years. Their hands, grinding and patting and laying the corn patties upon the hot metal, were a time machine. You could fly back to Tenochtitlán on their palms any day of the week.

They fed all us gawking kids. You could hang out at the tortillería and eat a pound of soft hot tortillas. They'd give them to us plain—good enough! Or they'd roll a few drops of lemon juice in one, or a pinch of salt, or both. I ate a couple of these mini-tacos while I waited.

They pulled pure white wrapping paper off a huge roll—just like my Grandpa's poetry roll—and tore off a foot or so and wrapped the tortillas snugly. The paper tucks were snug as diapers.

I headed home with the bundle hot and pulsing comfortably against my gut.

I stopped in the *botica*, the pharmacy/candy store/juju center/soda shop/icon seller/toy store, for a candy. My aunt knew I was going to steal some of her change. I was addicted to these rubbery, square banana-flavored Mexican candies. They tasted exactly like my mom's nail polish smelled. This was too marvelous, and I explored its ramifications every chance I got.

I was coming out, busy pulling the fillings out of my teeth, when Hugo caught up with me.

"Come on," he said.

"Where to?" I asked.

"Got to show you something."

"Tortillas," I said.

"They can wait," he said.

I followed him around the corner and up to the top end of the Rampa. I'd never been up there before. There was no reason to walk up there, and the car was too exhausted by the time it got to the house to go any farther. All it could manage was to turn around and fling itself back downhill.

We slipped between two houses. Down the hill. Into a small canyon.

"Where are we going?"

"I found something," he said.

We climbed up the narrowing arroyo. We stopped. He pointed.

There was a stairway. A big cement stairway. It flared a little at the bottom. It had railings. It went up about thirty steps. Then it ended. It went nowhere.

We stood on the bottom step and looked up it.

"Strange, huh?" he said.

"Yeah," I said. "And guess what. Somebody tied these two dogs together in the street."

V. Got the Devil in My Closet

Let me tell you about the demon before I go. You probably won't believe it. Gringos have a strangely difficult time with the bizarre details of the daily life of Latinos. People scoff at personal testimonials of wonders, but they love to read them in novels from Colombia. To us, however, magic realism is basically reality.

I'll admit, I have some trouble myself. A woman I knew in Tijuana inspected the rash on her husband's back and said:

"You're hungry for *chicharrones!*" (Fried pork rind.)

"No I'm not," he said.

"Yes you are," she insisted. "You have a craving for them."

"But I don't," he said.

"You do, but you just don't know it," she said. "That's why you got this rash—it looks like chicharrones."

He couldn't see it all that well, so he had to take her word for it.

What she did was, she boiled a bunch of chicharrones until they were soft, then she plastered the boiling slop onto his back. That the rash disappeared was taken to be a miraculous cure, though none of us suggested she had simply burned about three layers of skin off his back.

I can see where that's too magical. Chicharrón lust is silly. And the dreaded *agua de coco* is silly, too. It's a love potion made from menses and slipped into an unsuspecting man's coffee: When my relatives point out who put it in whose coffee to make him such a hapless love slave, I can laugh it off with the best of them. And when an extended family member's mother was caught in the middle of a black-magic incantation by her son, *and she had a pig's head instead of a human head,* I can, sort of, you know, ignore it.

Still, I'm not sure what to make of my Aunt Irma's bottle of holy water.

She told my father she'd been sensing the evil eye on him. Somebody had been shooting him the wicked mojo from a passing car, or some such nonsense. So, she had gone out to a shop and bought an evil-eye protector. It was a bottle of holy water tied up in a red velvet sack. She opened the sack and showed us the water: yes, we agreed, it was definitely a little bottle full of water. My father was to keep the bottle in his glove compartment, and it would soak up any evil eye fired his way.

My father, by the way, was not above crank ideas. For example, he wore a bracelet of magnets that supposedly sucked out all his ills through his wrists. Illness, arthritis, and impotence were all apparently cured by these miraculous magnets. Still, the holy water was too much. "Bullshit," he said when we got in the car. He threw it in the glove compartment and forgot about it.

Months later, of course, I opened the glove compartment looking for something else and found the pouch.

"Look, Dad!" I said.

We laughed.

I opened it.

The little bottle was full of black sludge. It looked just like old motor oil.

You figure it out!

In the downstairs second story, there was a small room. It was partially underground—its one grimy window looked out at ground level. Its roof was angled, and its floor was at least two feet above the level of the main rooms' floors. It was a dark anomaly in the northeast corner of the house. I could never figure out what my grandfather had in mind when he built it.

It was always rumored to have an evil presence. One of the items of evidence the family offered was that everyone who stayed downstairs ended up with some sort of respiratory illness. I, for example, got TB. The fact that a family of tubercular schoolgirls lived directly behind my bedroom didn't enter into the family myth.

The demon-in-the-backroom event didn't happen until after I was long gone, had come to the United States and the realm of reason. I was not there to witness any of it, so the whole story is secondhand. I took it on faith; you may not be able to.

Irma, the bowler aunt, and her sister, the farting aunt, teamed up to exorcise the foul being from the little room. They went to the Independencia church and filched some holy water, and they somehow procured some church incense—perhaps from my grandmother's extensive booty.

They went downstairs together, flinging droplets all over the place and blowing holy smoke in all the corners. They supposedly entered the room and demanded that the being leave. Then, they say with straight faces, they were physically picked up and thrown out.

All around them, the banana trees in the yard bore fruit; the neighbor's trapezoidal house refused to fall; Margo developed a marvelous skill for talking to birds—she could make them land on her fingers. Ernesto James ran out of bullets. Tijuana's Christmas decorations got fancier year by year, then grew old and faded and tattered. Margo moved away. Her mother moved away. The second first-story dogs grew old and died. In the street, a new generation of dogs got tied together to launch yet another generation of dogs. Hugo got married and had lovely daughters. My grandmother went dotty, once making the following announcement about me: "This man has a pee-pee this big!" Then, she died. Dope-fiend *cholos* crept into the darker corners and whispered curses at passersby. The tortilla shop's women were replaced by a machine. The botica stopped selling those chemical banana candies. The yellow castle faded to off-white, and there hasn't been a bear in sight for thirty years. And it never rains.

The saddest part is that they finally paved the Rampa. They made it easy to go there, and people who have not earned the hill traverse it blindly. Day and night, all manner of cars and trucks rush up and back, none of the drivers aware that they have come somewhere. They have crossed over into another, wilder, more beautiful land. A land that is now as invisible as its ghosts.

The Day I Launched

the Virgin Mary into Orbit

Logan Heights, in the early sixties, was already changing. They called it Shelltown. Someone said it was because of the old clamshells in the dirt in some sections of the neighborhood.

Racial tensions rose as the working-class white and Mexican population gave way to black families seeking housing. Apartment owners became slumlords seemingly overnight, moving in "colored" tenants, then refusing those tenants any of the basic services they expected. The whites and Mexicans saw the tide coming up National Avenue from the east and barricaded themselves, both emotionally and physically. We were fresh from Tijuana, part of the first tide that caused white families to hide, then flee. No one knew they were part of a cycle.

Street hassles became fairly common. I was thumped by black kids, singly and in groups, several times. Yet, it wasn't completely racial. They were going to the public school, but I was in my geeky St. Jude's Academy uniform—brown cords, white shirt, shiny black shoes, probably a red sweater. They saw my prim outfit and just couldn't help themselves.

Every morning, I tried to walk as slowly as possible on my way to the clutches of Sisters Martha-Ann and Paulana-Marie, girding myself for the daily observance of Mass in indecipherable Latin. Or, there was the torment of confession, when I'd have to kneel in the confessional and tell Father Sheridan anything I could think of. Hey, I was a sinner, but I was in second grade. Any sin of real value was years away. I knew he'd be happy if I'd been bad, but I had to make up sins: *Bless me Father, for I have sinned . . . uh . . . rude to Mom, and . . . uh . . . wanted to steal a candy bar . . . uh . . . rude to Mom?*

We were color-blind at St. Jude's. The black kids in there with us may have been as tough and bad-assed as the guys lying in wait for us on the street, but they all had to wear the same goofy outfit as the rest of us. The Chicano kids, just learning how bad-to-the-bone they could be, were also abashed by the outfits. How bad can you be in a bright red sweater? They had the double onus of being Catholic, something most of the black kids didn't have to worry about. The Chicanos, in their hearts yearning to be *vatos* along the lines of the grizzled ex-zoot-suiters in the neighborhood, were scared of the sisters. The sisters, after all, could ship 'em off to hell.

We gathered before the church, being barked, insulted, threatened, and hustled into raggedy lines by the sisters. I had recently informed Sister Martha-Ann that she was quite cute, thinking she would warm to the compliment. She did not. Now they had their eyes on me.

Inside, the Mass was interminable. Everybody hated kneeling especially; a few of us actually offered our suffering on our knees up to Jesus as a sacrifice. I spent almost every Mass equally split between a religious reverie and bored fantasy. Fancying myself some sort of boy Bernadette, I spent many accumulated hours mentally cajoling the plaster Christ on the cross to open his bloody eyes and look at me. The rest of the time, I was imagining how cool the church would look if a tidal wave came along and turned it upside down and washed it out to sea.

After Mass, we were herded to class. The girls, in their own uniforms—little white blouses, jumpers, knee socks— were insufferably holy. They sometimes agreed, probably telepathically, to hold up folded hands *en masse*, forming a smug line of prayerful saints. We boys couldn't help but cut up then: fart noises, giggling, and untucked shirttails swept us like a surge of demonic possession. Invariably, one or more miscreants fell into Sister Paulana-Marie's clutches. They were carted into the classroom and whipped with a yardstick. The truly evil girls would sit and watch the unfortunate boys dance in a galloping circle, one arm clamped in Paulana-Marie's grip, kicking and yelping as the yardstick cracked across their backsides.

Otherwise, school days in second grade were mostly composed of smuggled Monster trading cards and fat crayons that had one flat side to keep them from rolling off our desks. Aside from having my left-hand knuckles cracked with rulers to make me right-handed, and a bout of deep knee bends assigned when Paul Schnazzel and I were caught with plastic cars, things went pretty well. It was in third grade that I went bad.

It was their own damned fault.

In third grade, we were considered old enough to learn about the Rocky Path to Heaven, and the Superhighway to Hell. Holy cow—the road to heaven was gnarly in the extreme, a luridly painted narrow mountain road winding up steeply, and studded with boulders. Actually, it looked exactly like the street my grandmother lived on in Tijuana. In the meantime, the road to hell was a four-lane, rush-hour boogie, populated with porkpie-hatted partiers speeding to their doom in convertible Buicks.

Things had taken a turn.

Plus there was the slight problem of the Communists. Apparently, shoe-pounding Soviets and bearded Cubans were about to invade the nation. According to the good sisters, their main goal in life was to force us to renounce Jesus. *No!* we children protested. *They will torture you!* the nuns warned us. We were still somewhat firm in our faith, but wanted to know what, exactly, was this torture deal?

The Communists were planning—this must have come through the immense Nun Intelligence Agency—to drag us behind trucks until we said we hated Jesus.

The vatos decided they could take it. So we all joined in again: *We're with Jesus, Sister!*

Ah, but the Communists weren't just going to drag us down the street! Oh no! They were going to drag us over rough stones! Huge cobbles! (Wait—wasn't that the road to Heaven?) And they were going to do it until our skin was ripped off! We would be raw, aching meat! And all we'd have to do to stop it was say we hated Jesus.

Some of us began to consider the doctrine of divine forgiveness. He was supposed to forgive all sins, and we didn't like this bloody meat idea at all. We figured Jesus would just have to get over it.

The nuns would sometimes surprise us with gifts. I still have some of them. We'd be graced with small Christmas ornaments, little plastic mangers with glitter snow, Advent calendars with cool little red plastic windows, blue plastic rosaries with faux ivory crucifixes on them, various religious pictures—one of them featuring Jesus offering us his apparently surgically excised heart ringed with thorns.

But, on my worst day as a budding Catholic, it was hot and boring. I was in a snit because the knot of disinterested vatos and black boys in the back had discovered how to do pornographic drawings. They kept passing me a piece of paper with what appeared to be a bifurcated Y on it. "It's her weener!" one bonehead whispered.

Righteously, I marched up to the front of the room and handed it over. The nun's face went deep pink. She put the note away, but strangely didn't do anything. Returning to my seat, I was greeted with blood-thirsty stares. *It's payback time!* After lunch, the sister came up with one of her surprises. We each got a shrine of the Virgin Mother. It was a small plastic Virgin in a tan construction that looked like three Cadillac fins.

Somehow, the more the sister droned on about math that afternoon, the more the shrine began to look like Rocketship X-M. The little girl's hair in front of me looked more and more like a giant alien man-eating blob. My imaginary crewmen scrambled across the desktop, swarming into their ship, and she launched off. I basically imagined the Holy Mother as the crew compartment, while the shrine itself was the stabilizers and wings. I was having a swell time.

"Sister! Sister!" I heard one of the pornographers shout. "Luis is using the Virgin for a spaceship!"

"Am not!" I lied, Spaceship Virgin Mother held above the desk. I was piling on sin after sin at an alarming rate.

Suddenly, the sister rose like a black cloud from her desk. She didn't even look down as she reached for her ruler. All the rage within her—rage at the Communists, at the dirty note, at my sacrilege, filled her face. And she came. And I offered up the suffering in my butt to Jesus, while everyone around me sat and looked holy.

Down the Highway

with Edward Abbey

I'm driving Ed Abbey's Cadillac to Denver. It has moldered away in a dirt alley off Tucson's venerable main drag, and now it's going to reside in a pricey Republican enclave on the compromised high plains outside the mile-high city. Of course, if I told you which 'burb it was, I'd have to kill you.

A fire-engine-red '75 Eldorado, it has been parked for a year behind Ed's pal Buffalo Medicine's house, accumulating a thick coat of dust and a calligraphy of cat and raccoon tracks across its massive hood. The cables have fallen loose in the engine compartment, the generator's shot, weeds have choked the wheels, and the ragtop's in sad shape. Local writers cruise by occasionally, tip their gimme caps, raise a can of Coors, and drive away. Their wheels churn up the alley dirt, adding another layer of dust to the Caddie. Just like Ed's memory.

Buffalo Medicine has possibly rooked El Piloto, a devotee of the Abbeyite Order, by selling him the car for a price that might or might not be too much. Opinions vary. It all depends on where you're positioned in the continuing Ed debate. In Tucson, the debate is quite personal, since locals trade Ed sightings like baseball cards.

Ed Abbey—Sasquatch.

Along with the Ed sightings, we are confronted with the most peculiar facet of the Dead Ed Industry, the I-Was-Ed-Abbey's-Best-Friend Industry. Outside of Tucson, it's moderated a bit by distance into the I-Was-Ed-Abbey's-Biggest-Fan Industry. Shady dudes who may have tipped back a Dos Equis with Ed at a barbecue will now offer you insights into his soul, and a few of these Best Friends will offer to take Biggest Fans to Ed's "secret" grave site where more Dos Equis can be consumed. Of course, East Coast tenderfoots could be led to my backyard and told the mulch pile is Ed's grave, and they'd go home happy. I wonder how many people have stared at a thoroughly empty pile of dirt in Saguaro National Monument and said perfectly lovely things—into thin air. Nobody seems to find this behavior creepy.

It is a telling measure of the man, and all he accomplished, that so many are willing to define themselves by proximity—real or imagined—to his being.

How much would you pay for a piece of Ed Abbey? We are in a dicey period here, where shitheads Ed wouldn't

have spit on if they were burning buy his books and seven
Earth First! T-shirts and claim to be his soul mates. But El
Piloto, possibly as thorny and unsentimental a man as Ed,
has bought the car for love. I wonder what he'll do when
the Dead Ed Industry washes a bibliophile to his door with
a limp check for $28,000, dying to drive a piece of the myth.

What can I say? I stole Ed's pencil out of the car and am
hiding it in my office. That's a writer for you: a happy hypo-
crite.

One thing's for sure: Rudolfo A. Anaya won't be offering
anybody money for Ed's chariot. When he heard El Piloto
and I were motoring cross-country with it, he put a curse
on us. My cherished friend, Mr. *Bless Me, Ultima,* said: "I
hope you have four flat tires in the desert. I hope the car
catches fire. I hope it burns to the ground."

Way to go, Ed!

Making friends.

But I too am mad at Ed. I don't know why anybody else
is mad at him, and plenty of people are—which, of course,
in the post-Abbeyan universe, is all the more reason to love
Ed. That's part of the seductiveness of Edward Abbey, isn't
it? The world's full of bastards, and Ed will cuss them out
for us, tilt at them with his sharpened war lance, be in-
spected by the FBI, and occasionally blow up a bridge or
sodomize a tractor into submission, all the while throwing
cleverly hidden poems into his paragraphs and, for no ex-
tra charge, make us laugh.

We, in turn, get to feel like we have done battle with

wicked forces while hiding behind a dead man. We feel like Ed's pals. Ed speaks for us, we compliment ourselves by thinking. We say Ed is our voice, expressing our deep feeling, after Ed himself often set the agenda we now claim for our own in one of his books that we bought out of a "used" box for $1.45.

Chicano readers, too, could be seduced. Like many people with a cause, we can be essentially pathetic, eager to side with anybody who sounds halfway sympathetic. Our weariness with the struggle, our exhaustion, is what makes us vulnerable. Our exhaustion makes us latch on to a strong voice for justice. And Ed, with his championing of lizards and watersheds, seemed to be championing us, too. Ed made some of us hope. And we fell over like puppies, wagging and peeing at his feet.

This is proof enough for me that Ed was a great writer. He angers the effete, and he utterly seduces his readers into absorbing his pith as if we were amoebas. And, sometimes, he hurts us.

Edward Abbey once stuck a knife in my heart.

I didn't know him outside of his books, and although I ponder swiping the car now and then, I'm not going to claim any special connection to the man. Or the ghost. Connecting with the books was quite enough. *Desert Solitaire, The Monkey Wrench Gang, Black Sun, The Journey Home* all had a massive, perhaps catastrophic, effect on me. I went mad for Ed, but more important, and a major reason others fell in love with him too, was the aching love he ignited in me for the land. The world. The *tierra*.

Ed Abbey—shaman.

Imagine my shock, and the shock of all of Ed's other Chicano, Mexican, Hispanic readers when we picked up *One Life at a Time, Please* and read the now-infamous screed about ourselves, "Immigration and Liberal Taboos." In it, Ed sets down his official policies regarding Mexicans: "They come to stay and they stay to multiply." Or how about this *bon mot* from "egalitarian" Ed: "It might be wise for us as American citizens to consider calling a halt to the mass influx of even more millions of hungry, ignorant, unskilled, and culturally-morally-genetically impoverished people."

Morally, Ed? Culturally? This is a redneck hillbilly from Home, Pennsylvania. About people who had *culture* when his ancestors were dog-styling sheep and digging turnips and cow turds out of the sad mud in their serf villages. Of course, Ed also informed his readers that Latin American societies were societies of "squalor, cruelty, and corruption," while he was fast-approaching the stance that the American vista was one that was "open, spacious, uncrowded, and beautiful—yes, beautiful!"

Ed Abbey—Aryan.

Oh my, Ed, you lying bastard. After writing countless books in which you decry America as just the opposite of free and open, after doing that very thing in the same book, after seducing us with battle cries based on the very spoiling of this land by overcrowded gringo swine, you fall for Pete Wilsonesque scapegoating. The very prospect of living in a country teeming with brown cockroach people (to swipe Brown Buffalo's term) drives you into a hideous U-turn. The thought, apparently, of my people. The thought of me.

Did I remember to mention that writers are hypocrites?

Sitting in Ed's boat, Safeway parking lot, Broadway and Campbell, Tucson. The journey's about to begin. Two blueberry muffins and some styrofoam coffee for breakfast. My candidate for Miss Universe loads groceries into her whining little Coke-can car. Ed's Eldorado says: AMURCA FURST, BUDDEH! Ed's Eldorado does not say, "Earth first." If anything, it probably says, "Ed first." Hell yes. Ed's Eldorado remembers Pearl Harbor. The plates say HAYDUKE.

Ed's ghost sits in the back seat. He holds up his letter to the editor, *Arizona Daily Star,* January 1982: "I was not talking about 'cultural influences' but about the social and economic effects of unchecked mass immigration from the impoverished nations to our south, particularly Mexico. Certainly Mexico has contributed much to the Southwestern heritage; I like tacos, tequila, and *ranchero* music about as much as anybody else does."

Tacos? Tequila? The thing about ghosts is, they don't have to stop at putting their feet in their mouths. They can go ahead and gobble the whole leg, jam it in there all the way down till they've maneuvered their heads up their own asses.

By the way, Ed says in the introduction to *One Life at a Time, Please* that "Immigration and Liberal Taboos" is his favorite essay in the book.

Did Ed Abbey hate Mexicans? Or was he really setting out to tweak liberals? I'm trying hard not to do back flips here just to defend my favorite writer. Consider: where many writers have a pitiable need to be loved, Ed seemed to have a puzzling need to be reviled. Puzzling, that is, if one considers Ed Abbey to be merely a *writer*. We all know he was an anarchist, a trickster, an agitator, and an "eco-warrior," whatever that means. In his "A Writer's Credo" (same book), the very first sentence says: "It is my belief that the writer should be and must be a critic of the society in which he lives." Not a word about fame, love, beauty, or literary awards.

Ed Abbey, by his own words, saw himself as a critic, a gadfly. In McGuane's words, "the original fly in the ointment." And nobody was spared. After all, *One Life at a Time, Please* contains his even more infamous assault on "The Cowboy and his Cow."

Perhaps it should not surprise me then, when in the middle of my outrage over this awful essay, I stumble on a sentiment that I absolutely agree with. Ed suddenly says: "The conservatives love their cheap labor; the liberals love their cheap cause. (Neither group, you will notice, ever invites the immigrants to move into their *homes*. Not into *their* homes!)"

Right on, Homey! El Vato Loco Cactus Eddie y Qué Abbey, Barrio Desierto Rifa Con Safos Cabrones, lays down some righteous *chingazos* for *la causa, Ese*!

Oh, well.

Some of us are social misfits; we spend vast periods of time locked in rooms banging at typewriters and computers. Those of us who like to write "outdoors" stuff spend even more hours stumbling over rocks and backing into cacti. Alone. Worse if a writer has a cause. We will burrow through bystanders as if they were dirt clods and we were rabid moles. Of all the things I could say about Ed, I suspect that nobody would accuse him of being a schmooze-meister.

Indelicacy follows us through our tunnels. Chicanos, we must admit, have said scabrous and wounding things about gabachos in publication after publication. Mexicans say foul things about both gringos and Chicanos. The whole lot of us can cast a suspicious eye toward Central America and points south.

And, of course, writers carry the baggage of their times, their origins, and their own spiritual and intellectual laziness.

I admire Edward Abbey. I enjoy his books. And I love his bad-taste car—all the way down to its honky-tonk-red carpet on the dash. This car is twenty steel feet of Ed's laughter.

I also decry his ignorance and his duplicity.

Guess what? Ed Abbey had feet of clay.

Just like me.

Still, he managed to throw in a closing that has resonated with me all through the years. I knew, in a terribly clear way, that he was right. "Stop every campesino at our southern border, give him a handgun, a good rifle, and a case of ammunition, and send him home. He will know what to do with our gifts and good wishes. The people know who their enemies are."

Ed's ghost lights a cigar and puts its feet up on the seat back. I ponder this last paragraph as we cross the Luna County line. A million acres of open desert accrues paper cups and PayDay wrappers around us. Flat as a griddle for a few miles, then truculent upheavals of bare naked mountains. To the north, grape-juice rainclouds color the horizon.

Indians and Chicanos, who know a good thing when they see it, catch up to the car and give us the big thumbs-up.

Ed Abbey—lowrider.

Whores

It's south of Tijuana and about an hour inland from the sea. It lies on the western lip of the town, near a small cemetery and the old rail line. The town itself is a classic rural Mexican community, cobble and dirt streets, a small square with a gazebo, and such new developments as marijuana and *cholos* and graffiti. Sometimes gringos make their way here, but few stick around long enough to be impressed. Once in a while, they even make their way to this place, called El Club Papagayo Para Hombres. The Parrot Club for Men.

It's not as exciting or evil-hearted as some of the places in Tijuana. Most of the clients here are skinny farmhands or well-fed minor urban functionaries or fat off-duty cops.

A few of the women are too old for work in a more fancy house, and the other ones are just lucky that this is as far down as they'll go.

It's a big structure, and it presents a blank wall to the street. Concrete blocks are slathered over with slapdash Mexican stucco and a green paint job was touched up in the 1950s. The relentless sun has faded it a sort of watercolor yellow. If you listen at the wall at night, you will hear the forced sounds of partying emanating from within— trumpets, laughter, jukeboxes, bad live *rocanrol*. And the women, every night, can be heard shouting naughty jokes and risqué insults.

I am in a car with the most macho young men of the extended Urrea family. Men I first met years ago when my father decided I was "queer." Third grade, perhaps. Tough Mexican boys brought up to the United States because I was being raised gringo. I was speaking Spanish in too *pocho* a manner: not enough rough edges in the words, not enough disdain and wit inherent in my pronunciation. My *r*'s were not hard enough, the *g* and *j* sounds lacked the heft of phlegm at the back of the palate to really sizzle. I had learned, to my utter shock, that the wrong emphasis on the wrong consonants could lead to humiliation, insults, even violence. I remember one of these men giving me tequila in the fifth grade, then cigarettes, in order to roughen the far borders of my words. I apparently had a garden on my tongue, and the men were demanding a desert.

They were doubly worried about me because I had made the deadly error of announcing in the first grade that I wanted to be a priest. My father said, "But you won't want to have women." What did I know of women? I'd have visions of the plaster Christ on the cross opening His eyes and looking at me. I wanted the stigmata. I wanted to work miracles and save the sick. "You want to wear a black dress? You'll be a faggot!"

"What's that?" I remember wondering.

Outside the whorehouse, looking like they've been beamed up from 1970, a small group of Mexican males gathers nervously. They're mostly young, but one of them is too young. Fathers regularly bring their sons to the Parrot Club for their first sexual encounter. The cop at the door smiles like an uncle when a terrified twelve-year-old comes under the wing of his dad. But solo, you'd have to be at least eighteen. And one of these boys is only fourteen. But he's tall and without his glasses, he looks maybe old enough.

They have gathered to buy him his first sex.

Their names are Grillo, Fausto, El Gordo, Fu Manchu, and Blondie. Blondie's other nickname is Pigfoot. But tonight, his lighter hair is more visible than his stubby feet. He's the fourteen-year-old.

It is a law: Mexican males must have nicknames. Grillo, in this group, is called El Red. There are others in their circle known as Dracula, Frankenstein, Taras Bulba, and El Chino Cochino. (The dirty Chinaman—he's one of the many Mexican-Chinese who inhabit the Norte.) The best nickname in town belongs to a man they all fear. He's called El Quemapueblos, and I agree that it's the best nickname

I've ever heard. Its pithiness can't be translated into En-
glish. The best I can do is The Man Who Burns Down Cit-
ies.

Thank God he doesn't figure into this story, I think.

My father imported these strange, rangy boys to inten-
sify the manhood factor around the house. One of them—
I'll call him The Bull, a nickname he was awarded for the
size of his penis—was a fighter and an athlete. Something I
definitely was not. In my memory, The Bull is ten feet tall
and muscular, evil, self-satisfied enough that he even sleeps
with a smirk. Years later, wandering into the whorehouse, I
realize with a start that he's just a minor little bureaucrat.
Another God-damned wise guy picking the meat off the
bones of the poor, sliding illegal funds sideways into his
various bank accounts. He has matted hair, weasely eyes,
and dresses like a character from an old episode of *Charlie's
Angels*. All petroleum-product materials. He's shorter than
I am.

I start to laugh.

"What?" he says, half smiling, but worried there's a joke
somewhere that he's not in on, already partially angry that
I might be laughing at him, when it has always been his
right to take ferocious aim at me.

"I could break your neck," I tell him, "with one hand."

His face flushes.

His blush, in Club Papagayo's frosty tube light, looks
purple.

The Bull's legendary good looks have rotted and turned the color of half-cooked liver.

We have all gathered for a family holiday. The Bull's family home is stately by village standards.

Over supper he has told me, "We've got to go to the *bule* tonight. They've got a deaf-mute girl!"

He beams at this news—it's the most exciting thing he's thought of all day. I can only suppose it's the exotic nature of it that has him in a lather. It's the only new thing to do in town except for the movie theater, which is showing John Wayne's old nugget, *The War Wagon*, dubbed into German with Spanish subtitles. As we talk, hundreds of little birds tumble through the air like leaves on a sidewalk.

"She's even cute," he enthuses. "and she charges 30,000 pesos."

At the current exchange rates, I'm thinking, what—ten bucks at most.

"Just," he says, "don't tell my wife we went."

I'm not telling anyone anything. It's my plan to get him in the graveyard and beat him senseless. I feel the rocks in my hands; I hide them under the table. I want to bury him alive out there, pour dirt in his mouth, listen to him under ground as the scorpions descend.

We follow the boys inside. I feel like Blondie's father. He could be me at fourteen. The entrance is off a small courtyard. Around this courtyard are six shacks. On the front step of one, a child plays.

"Whores' houses," my host quips.

"They live here?"

"You can't expect them to go into town! They keep to themselves."

A river of shit has run out of the spectacularly noxious toilets near the door. We all make our crossing in single file. The open door of the Parrot Club belches smoke and discordant electric guitar. Too metaphorical. A cop stops the boys and frisks them. He doesn't even look at Blondie. They're in.

I grab a table near them and look around.

Three women are visible. The deaf-mute, who is heartbreakingly cute, has a short hairdo with no makeup. She is using a crude sort of sign language to indicate lust to a table full of drunk men. She grabs her crotch, makes a pained face, writhes. She pantomimes masturbation as the farmers giggle like little boys and poke each other with hard black forefingers. I see childhood in her face. Dolls and Popsicles. She looks like she's selling lemonade at a sidewalk stand in La Jolla. And masturbating.

The other woman has a face like a friendly turtle and a brassy voice that brays louder than anything in the room. My host asks, "Are you mute, too?"

She points to her ass.

"This isn't mute!" she reports. "It cuts loud farts!"

She smiles at me.

"*Hola, guapo,*" she says.

"Good evening, señorita," I reply.

She stares at me like I've said something exceedingly strange. Stops smiling.

The Bull tries to touch her, and she yanks her arm away.

She starts to dance with a small ranchero. They look like the two ends of a horse having a seizure. The song is a Mexican version of "Rock Lobster." Some idiot on the record is bellowing: "*Langosta! Langosta Rock!*"

The third woman, the one the young boys at the next table have obviously come for, is terrifying. She's Tina Turner—even has the same wig. Her massive eyelashes are the size and shape of tarantulas. When the boys goad Blondie into touching her—he timidly taps her on the arm with one finger—she glares at him. I'd swear she's hissing. He pulls his hand away fast and looks at the floor.

"Ay ay ay!" they say.

The Bull and his invasionary force came into my life with a promise of companionship and adventure. I was a Boy Scout. The Scouts were the only escape from the eternal race war between my gringo mother and my *mejicano* father. It was also the only way I, raised on dirt and outhouses and barrio sadism, could hike up a mountain, see coyotes, drink from waterfalls. The vatos informed me that Boy Scouts were pussies.

If I really wanted to be *un hombre,* I'd learn to box.

Then they slapped me silly. I learned fast that my bloody noses were *funny.* I was supposed to wipe the blood off on my forearm and laugh.

I also learned an unspoken lesson about machismo.

Some of the toughest males, *muy macho chingones*, seemed obsessed with forcing younger children to suck their dicks. Each one wanted to push his hard-on up the asses of young boys and girls. These men who were to rescue me from the unforgivable queerness of serving God wanted to ride the backs of little boys. Little boys like me.

Beside the bar there is a small shrine to the Virgin of Guadalupe. Votive candles burn at her feet, and some wilted carnations are strewn at the statue's sandals. The center of the room is a big concrete dance floor. The walls all have two doors. They are so cheap that you could, if you really wanted to, look through the slats and watch the action inside.

Each door opens into a small room. In each room, one bed and one chair. One small table holds a bowl and a jug of water, a bar of soap, and a rag. Above the beds hang crucifixes.

Once, the police captain of the town fell in love with a woman who worked here. He got so jealous—and drunk on tequila—that one night he burst into the Club Papagayo, kicked open her door, and shot her and the unfortunate beer salesman on top of her. The Parrot Club didn't know what to do with the room. They considered closing it in honor of the tragedy, but ultimately changed the mattress and went on as usual.

The deaf girl—she can't be more than eighteen, I've decided—comes up to me and offers me the brother handshake. We clench hands. She looks like one of my English students. But suddenly, she gets a flushed expression, then pantomimes something going up her. She stands there and grinds at my table, hands on crotch. She's doing her little dance for me now. The Bull punches me on the arm and laughs appreciatively. Then she opens her eyes and grins at me and nods. I shake my head. She has dimples. She points at me, at my crotch, then holds her hands about two feet apart and makes an "Ooh" with her mouth.

I shake my head.

I laugh.

I hold up two fingers and hold them about one inch apart and look sad. This cracks her up. She shakes my hand and rushes off to the next table. "You had her," my host says. "You could have fucked her up the ass!"

The man with the macho box comes around to the boys' table.

He's called El Maestro, the master, as are all workmen in the places where the old Mexican ways are still practiced. Mexico is rapidly becoming as rude as the United States, but in courtlier days, mastery was honored. Shoeshine boys, barbers, or violin virtuosos were all maestros. And this maestro brings the macho box, a device known to anyone foolish enough to hang out in Mexican bars very long.

It's basically a torture device. A box with a couple of dials, a trillion batteries inside, and wires attached to two metal rods. For some reason, Mexican men can't resist holding these rods and trying to prove how much shock they can withstand. Think of it: the maestro actually gets paid to turn his knobs and torture men—and the torturees are the ones who pay! The really brilliant maestros offer, as a prize, free shocks. This is pure capitalism at its best.

Blondie has been anesthetized by his first serious gulps of tequila. He has confided to me what his friends don't know—he's too afraid of Tina Turner to try to make love to her. His buddies hook him to the machine and the maestro cranks it up. Blondie hangs on. After a while, he *has* to hang on because his fists are cramped onto the rods. "Not. So. Bad," he says. His arms curl and rise above his head. The maestro really lets him have it. But he can't give up now—everybody, even Tina, is watching. His knuckles clack together above and behind his head. He is either smiling or frozen in an electrified rictus.

The turtle-faced woman comes up to me.

"Writer," she says, "look at this."

I put down my notebook and look up.

The Bull says, *"Pinche maricón. Puto. Joto.* Writing in your little diary all night."

A beer delivery man has been pestering me. He is overwhelmed with drunken filial love, you know—the kind that immediately precedes a mass slaying. He shakes my hand about ten times, hanging on my table, insisting, *"Tú, amigo mío."*

The turtle-faced woman cuts him off and pulls a Polaroid print out of her blouse. In it she's standing there naked.

Smiling like she's in front of the flamingo exhibit at the zoo. Her nipples are black.

"For you," she says, "500 pesos."

The Bull announces, "I love this shit!"

Over at the next table, Blondie has followed his macho box challenge with a drinking contest with a local stud named Mauser, after the German rifle. I never ask, but I draw my own conclusions. He wins 700 pesos on an impromptu bet as he and Mauser chug tequila from eight-ounce tumblers. I will later learn that Blondie will spend the night with his head in a plastic bucket, convinced his bed, uplifted by demons, is flying around the room. He will beg Jesus, in the classic drunk's prayer, to sober him up, and he will *never drink again.*

With the winnings, and the money pitched in by the boys, Blondie's got about enough for sex.

Tina whips her wig in the near distance, curls her lip, goes "Chk" with her mouth to show her disdain. But keeps her eye on him.

I watch Blondie. He's breaking out in a sweat, and it's not just the booze. Fu Manchu is almost asleep. He's lost his bridge somewhere, and his upper lip blows in and out of his mouth like laundry on a line. Fausto is fairly sober; Grillo is doing cricket imitations with his mouth. El Gordo hates his nickname. Who'd want to be called "Fatso?" His real name is Roberto.

He leans over to Blondie and makes a drunken confession: "You're lucky," he says, "to have so much love from these guys."

"What do you mean?" says Blondie.

"You're only fourteen!" Roberto cries. "I am twenty-one! And *I've never been laid!*" He bangs the table.

Blondie is no fool. I can see it in his face. Inspiration.

"Boys," he says. "Boys!"

They drag their attention away from the dance floor, where everyone is wiggling around to "EL Farolito."

"I love you all," says Blondie. "I do."

Drunken promises of undying love and brotherhood come from their lips in response.

"I love it that you have brought me here and given me this."

He shows them the money.

They agree that they have given it to him.

"But brother Roberto here." He touches El Gordo. "My dearest friend."

They take it in stride—in Mexico, when you're drunk, everybody's your dearest friend or deadliest enemy. Roberto, through the magic of intoxication, is suddenly *everybody's* dearest friend.

"Fucking Gordo," they say.

"And Roberto is twenty-one years old to my fourteen!"

This is clearly Blondie's Gettysburg Address. He will, I suspect, live longer in the town's mythology for this act than anything having to do with Tina Turner.

"And Roberto is a virgin!"

"No!" they say as Roberto hangs his head in sorrow.

"It's true," Roberto says.

"I," Blondie says, "have time. Roberto does not."

He's a hero! The boys can't believe his loyalty to El Gordo. They buy him a beer and slap him on the back. One of them signals for Tina. She storms across the dance floor at them, looking like she's going to slap somebody. They push Roberto at her. He holds out the money. She takes it, sinks her nails into his forearm, and pulls him away.

The little door slams.

As we leave, the deaf prostitute signs something that I can't figure out. She repeats her gestures until I understand. She is saying: "I want to come with you."

The Bull says, "You're not writing about me, are you?"

"Yes," I say, smiling.

"What?" he demands.

I continue to smile.

Bloody noses are funny, after all.

"Oye, *cabrón*," he warns.

"I only," I whisper, "write the truth, you son of a bitch."

He moves away from me.

Outside, the boys wait for Roberto. When he finally comes out, his hair is a mess. He looks very sad. As they walk away, he keeps looking back at the Club Papagayo.

The little prostitute tugs at my arm. She gestures at herself, at me, away, to the north. She places her hands before her heart, as if she were praying. Her eyes are wet.

"Don't tell my wife about this," The Bull pleads.

My God—he's terrified of his wife. The top of his head

reaches my nose. I look into the dark—the cemetery wall is barely visible across the road. A thousand dogs are barking at the moon. I put my hand on the back of his neck. It's skinny. I imagine the blows. I squeeze lightly. He winces.

"Do you remember when we were boys?" I ask.

His eyes, huge with worry, rotate in their sockets. Are they looking for escape? Then they settle on my face.

"We had fun, right?" he says.

"Not really."

The color is draining from his face.

I hug him.

He relaxes against me.

"You taught me to be a man," I say into his ear. I hug him harder. "I'm a writer now," I remind him. "And I will make you famous." I slap him on the back. "I don't need to kill you. I can make you immortal."

He pulls away.

"Qué?" he says.

"All of you. Every bit of you, *Bull*."

I push him away.

I walk out the gate.

She is watching me. He stands between her and me. The boys are laughing in front of me. Roberto is talking quietly. As I catch up to them, he says, "Do you think she would go out on a date with me?"

I stop halfway between the graveyard and the whore-house. The Bull is running toward me. The little whore turns and walks back inside. The boys move away, gray as ghosts. I can hear them, laughing at Roberto all the way home.

Sanctuary

Mamá Chayo saved my life. She allowed her husband, the mighty Abelino, to believe he had saved me. But that is the way powerful Mexican women work their medicine, they let their men playact and strut and believe they run the world. Healing, though—that has a woman's face.

I had come out of Tijuana ragged and skinny and fighting for life. I was three years old, and I had already survived German measles, intestinal infections, chronic bronchial infections, and scarlatina. By the time we crossed the line into the United States, I had a skin ailment that was eating bloody gashes into my private parts. And I had tuberculosis.

Our good neighbors in that poor 1958 barrio wanted to help. But I, tucked into the corners of couches, coughed like a tiny Doc Holliday. They had children, too, and they became convinced that I would infect them all, and they reluctantly banned me from their homes.

My parents both had to work. They were desperate for some place to park me. The situation was hopeless, which of course is when miracles are supposed to happen.

My father was working one of the many tiresome and depressing menial jobs that would occupy his attentions for the rest of his new American life—bread truck driver, busboy, bowling alley attendant. In 1958, he had a job canning tuna at the big cannery on the edge of San Diego Harbor. My aunts got him the job. He stood in his spot on the line from seven in the morning till six at night. Sometimes he'd move off the conveyer belts and gut fish with the steel blades on long pole handles. Tuna the size of sheep swung toward him on hooks. He zipped them open: pale blood dripped off his rubber apron and soaked into his cuffs and his socks. My father used to come home at night smelling of fish. All through my childhood cannery workers who radiated fish stink seemed to lurk in every third corner with their white nurse shoes stained pink.

Abelino worked in the slot beside my father. Perhaps it was the smell that broke down the barrier between them. Perhaps it was the wearying racket of the machinery. Maybe it was just the numbing boredom of belts delivering an unending flow of shredded flesh to them. But my father, overcoming his natural sense that Urreas were somehow superior to other Mexicans, especially rustic Mexicans, began a friendship with Abelino. I believe it was Abelino's iron-hard bearing that won my father's respect. His face looked like it was carved from oak. To look at him, you'd think his bones were older than time, old enough to be rusty within him. He had hands like great paddles. And when he spoke, you were hearing nineteenth century Mexico.

The language he used had disappeared from "polite" discourse. His was a rural speech, punctuated by hillbilly phrases: the bathroom, for example, was *el escusado*—the excuse-me. Instead of using the proper word for "like this," or "that way"—*así*—he used a word left over from the 1700s: *asina*. His pronunciations were wrong, according to my father. In place of the proper name of milk—*leche*—Abelino spoke the dear country man's word—*lechi*. And, in place of telling someone they were dirty, or needed to wash their hands, he used the bumpkin's phrase, *estás puerco*—"You're pig."

He was a pearl diver from the surreal desert shores below La Paz, Baja California. He had come north for reasons he didn't care to explain, hauling his wife and children with him. His wife, Rosario, was nicknamed Chayo. She knew the old ways of the herbs and the roots. My father would come to think of her as an Indian woman, though he would never think to ask her about her background. Her skin was dark, a lovely shade of brown. Her eyes and hair were dark, and she wore her braided tresses in a tight bun at the back of her head. She wore cat-eye glasses, and she was small, and she covered her mouth when she laughed, and her feet were splayed and flat. She too was from the deserts of La Paz. To a mainlander like my father in those days, La Paz was the mysterious wilderness. Timbuktu. And the Indian old ways were both fearsome and wondrous. Maybe that was what caught his attention.

And the mystery of my father's whiteness and refined ways on the fish canning line must have intrigued Abelino, but like my father, he would never be so rude as to ask. One day at lunch, or as they shared a cigarette on a five-minute break on the docks, my father finally confessed to Abelino that his boy was sick. This would have been hard for him— both he and my mother were ashamed of my tuberculosis. My mother called it a ghetto disease. A sickness of the filthy and the poor. Such insults as "lunger" had still been in use when she was a girl. My father considered it a disease of *peones* and prostitutes. Still, he told Abelino how frantic he was getting with no one brave enough to help him. And Abelino, a fearless man, said, "We'll take him."

They called my privates *el tilichi*. Mamá Chayo and the womenfolk of the house who bathed me and put their green powders on me kidded me for years about the sorry state of that region when they first saw it. "Your poor tilichi," Mamá would say, "was falling off. But we stuck it back on for you!" Her twin daughters laughed uproariously as they hid their faces and blushed and cried, *"Ay, Mamá."*

This is how the rescue operation developed. Father would bundle me up at dawn while my mother was still slowly rising in her bedroom. He'd carry me out to his beloved '49 Ford, and he'd sit behind the wheel and tuck me in behind the great barrel of his upper body. There, upright and wrapped tight in my magic blanket, I'd cough into his ribs as he drove. Later I'd learn to stand there, wedged in against him. Once as we drove to Mamá Chayo's house, we saw a waterspout furling up out of the South Bay, as terrifying and crooked as the twister in *The Wizard of Oz*. It was in black and white, unlike the Technicolor garden that surrounded their house.

Abelino would be waiting on the steps of their porch, surrounded by geraniums. Mamá had bred her own strains—one of them had navy blue flowers with sky blue edges. And when we'd pull up, the women would rush out and flow down the steps and steal me from Dad's arms. He and Abelino would drive off together, and I would be carried into the holy shadows of 420 West Twentieth Street. There I'd stay until nightfall, when my father would trade Abelino in for me, and we'd go back home.

As 1958 turned to 1959, it became obvious that I wanted to be at West Twentieth Street more than I cared to be at home, so the daily routine expanded to weekend visits. I'd live with Mamá Chayo and her family from Friday morning until Sunday night. After a couple of years, preschool and kindergarten consumed my days. I always hated school, even college. Thinking back on it now, I believe I always knew that my days would be better spent hiding in the garden, stealing grapes, learning to dance with the twins, making pathetic tortillas that always—no matter how I concentrated—came out looking like underpants.

And by the time I started my sleepovers, Mamá Chayo had cured me of every disease.

How do you tell a story that cannot be told?

I tried to explain the simple story of Mamá Chayo's house for twenty years. I found that as a writer, I had to back into the facts. I had to hide the story in poems, as though art could have somehow delivered me to truth. Then I buried the story in fiction: the García family and home that takes up the last third of my novel *In Search of Snow* is based on West Twentieth Street.

Things still seemed full of wonder in that house. Perhaps it was because I was still so young, though Mamá Chayo was already old and her capacity for wonder was not diminished. Maybe it was the time—maybe the millennium is too late a date for small miracles. But I can still remember when mundane things had a glow about them, as if they were part of some process of revelation. Like the day I first ate sliced bread. I can't believe that I, tapping away at a laptop computer while the CD changer cycles through Chemical Brothers remix disks can remember the first slices of Wonder Bread I ever saw. Mamá Chayo committed that particular miracle, emerging from the pantry with this soft white stuff covered with grape jelly and peanut butter—*la pinah battah*. After a lifetime of tortillas and occasional *bolillo* rolls, I was flabbergasted. They didn't call it "Wonder" for nothing.

The relentless contrast between West Twentieth and my small apartment in the 'hood certainly made the enchantments of the garden more vivid. At home, I was under siege from angry neighbors and scary vatos outside, and the parental jihad within. The weather report for the inside of our apartment: shadowy, with growing areas of darkness. At Mamá Chayo's house, however, everyone was loved. Period. There was always enough love to go around. Nobody was too tired, too angry, too depressed, or too "tipsy" to love.

By love, I don't mean drippy sentiment. Nobody at West Twentieth made goo-goo eyes at anyone else. Love, in that house, was a bedrock fact, not discussed nor fretted over, never analyzed and barely recognized. Love simply *was*. There is a way in which a family rises in the morning that says *love*. There is a way in which a family shares one bathroom that says *love*. There is even a way in which a cup of coffee at three o'clock on a slow and rainy day says *love*.

Sure, they got cranky. They got fed up. They hollered at me. I was, after all, a boy. As a boy, I was fully endowed with all pertaining boyish idiocies, manias, noises, funks, stampedes, stinks, and questionable behaviors that would lead any sensible adult to shout. Abelino even cursed at me in florid and operatic recitatives. But, without fail, they loved.

Mamá Chayo and Abelino had been married forever, and they still loved each other enough that they could love everybody else. True love seems to be a spiritual loaves and fishes: it doesn't get used up, but keeps regenerating itself to feed all comers. Maybe that is what religious books really mean when they bandy about such terms as "living water." I think it fills up your heart, then it starts to overflow and water everyone else's.

Sharing their home with them were their twins, Quela

and Fina. My first sweethearts. My older women. Quela, the sorrowful one, went out every day to clean houses. Fina, the sunny one, stayed home every day to clean the one house. I pursued Fina relentlessly, fascinated by the world of the women. Occasionally, a ranchera song came on the radio that was so rabid in its accordion raving that Fina would cast away her broom, and we'd dance like maniacs all over the living room while Mamá Chayo cackled. We were especially fond of the shark song (*"Tiburón, tiburón— Tiburón a la vista. . . ."*) that would get us booty-shaking in a fashion that Abelino would have exploded over if he wasn't outside killing termites or building giant wooden Stars of David to hold up his Christmas lights.

And Quela, so mysterious when she returned home from those strangers' houses, so tired and beautiful in her sleepiness, wearing the strange magic of *el lipisticky* and *el polvo*— makeup. I would watch her etch in the lines around her eyes, watch her hit herself in the face with her powder puff. She even let me watch her snap her stockings to her garter once. I thought I'd faint. Sometimes I'd sneak into her room and taste her lipstick, playing make-believe that she was kissing me.

On Saturdays, her day off, Quela would sit at the work table in the kitchen and sort the beans. This sounds far less enchanting than it was: her graceful hands with their slightly long nails moved like a dance over the surface of the table. The pinto beans, hard and clacking like dominoes, swirled and skipped beneath her fingers. Without looking, Quela could spread and scatter hundreds of beans, all the while flicking out broken and rotten beans, sliding aside twigs and pebbles. At the same time, as if she'd grown a third hand, she was swooshing the good beans into the cooking pot she held in her lap.

Both sisters made flour tortillas every day. I attended the tortilla-making each day as if it were a religious ceremony. It was, clearly, an ancient ritual. Every morning, from the days of Aztecs making their *tláxcaltin,* Mexican women made tortillas. My father, an avid history buff, pointed this out to me. Quela or Fina would assemble the materials: flour, water, lard. Rolling pins, the aluminum tub, clean cotton cloths. They'd mix and knead and then make dough balls, and the dough balls would be sprinkled with a dust of white flour, and then the rolling pins would hit the dough traveling in the shape of a cross, and somehow the ball of dough with two hard passes of the rolling pin would be transformed into a perfect droopy disk. Whichever one was not creating the tortillas would transfer the raw dough onto a heated flat pan, where she'd use a wadded-up cloth to gently pop the blisters that rose in the dough as it cooked.

My own family, from the south, ate only corn tortillas. To them, maize was the only acceptable tortilla-making material. You could divide all of post-revolutionary Mexico along the *maíz/harina* line. Corn tortillas are Emiliano Zapata. Flour tortillas are Pancho Villa.

No matter what kind of dough they eat, however, all Mexicans from those days before machines made their tortillas have recorded within them the sacred rhythm of ten million women passing life through their hands. Their palms drummed out a steady cadence that set the background beat for the music of laughter, gossip, coughing, arguments; all around the beat there played the melody of frying, of pots clanging, of knives chopping, of water and plates and cups and spoons ringing. The sound of their palms as natural to us as a heartbeat: *pit-pat . . . pit-pat . . . pit-pat . . . pit-pat.*

Nina was usually asleep.

She was the fabulous old one who commanded the sewing room at the side of the house. It was on her old iron bed from the turn of the century, tucked in behind her sewing machine, that I slept. She had been taken in by Abelino many years before I was born, and she was the twins' godmother, Abelino and Mamá's *comadre*—co-mother. And in turn, Abelino and Mamá became my godparents, officiating at my baptism at Our Lady of Guadalupe, thus becoming my parents' *compadres*. We were all, by this marvelous ritual, made family.

Nina was ancient. I'd sit at her feet, toying with her huge, blocky, black old-woman shoes as she slowly wearied of sewing or crocheting, and her hands would dip slowly, and she'd nod, and her eyes would slowly close, and the white whiskers on her chin would tremble as she started to snore. Nowadays, I suppose, she would be recognized as the Crone, the storehouse of female wisdom. To me, she was the source of mystery, and in that home, mystery was a comfort. I never knew if she'd ever been married, or had children, or even if she too had come from La Paz. I couldn't even imagine if she'd ever been young. Nina was ninety-five years old for at least twenty years. And she was the ambassador of old age: being ancient seemed to mean that you went to the dreamlands to do your work. You remembered things nobody else knew anymore, and you saw people in your mind who had been gone longer than those around you had been alive. Nina heard everyone's confessions, and she laughed weakly at everyone's jokes—when she laughed, she sounded like she was sobbing.

Her hair was a nimbus of white cotton, and her cane—which seemed like a forbidden thing of power, an object of awe—was dark wood. Her magic wand and her weapon. She once battered a purse snatcher over the head with it when she could still perambulate around the neighborhood. As time rolled on, Nina could only move from her bedroom to the sewing room and back to the living room to watch television. She rocked as she walked, heavily swinging back and forth while her cane thumped on the floor.

And she spoke Chinese. At least we called it Chinese. We'd beg and beg her to do it, whatever kids were gathered together, and finally she'd poke us with her cane and start spouting her gibberish: "Hoki-choki-choy! Boya-choya-moy!" It was only after she was gone that I started to wonder if it was, in fact, gibberish. What if she was saying something else? What if she was speaking from deep within her mystery—some tongue half forgotten, some language abandoned as she fled the revolution? What if it wasn't Chinese at all, but some mother tongue like Otomi, or Tarahumara, or Apache, or Yaqui? What if Nina sang her song and it was doomed to go out forever unheard?

English troubled no one at West Twentieth. Mamá Chayo engaged in long, warm phone conversations with my mother that consisted largely of pidgin English, pidgin Spanish, some sort of customized Swahili, and a lot of giggles, "uh-huhs," and humming. Neither Mamá nor Nina could pronounce Phyllis, Mom's name, so they happily mangled it into various permutations: Doña Pillips, Señora Feliza, La Prips. Abelino delighted in learning good English cuss words; otherwise why did he need English? God's name in vain, in his mouth, became a cry in an alien tongue: Cheezakrytes! Oh Gadammah! And Quela and Fina, who had reason to deal with the outside world more than their elders, created soundscapes that reasonably approximated English, kinds of songs that echoed messages that the Americanos spoke. "Hi," Fina would say. "Fau-va-ju?" And the Americano would say, "I'm fine, thank you." And Fina would laugh and nod at everything the Americano said thereafter.

Nina and Mamá Chayo, barely understanding a lick of what was said, were driven out of their minds by the American soap operas that came on every afternoon. Their favorite was *Edge of Night*, though they had no idea what the title meant. They didn't even bother trying to mispronounce it. They identified the show by the name of their favorite character, Jessie.

"It's time for la Jessie, Comadre!" Mamá would shout.

Nina would snort awake saying, "Oh, la Jessie!" and she'd struggle out of her chair and thump out to her personal corner of the living room. She sat in a rocker beside the table that held the Catholic saints, the photographs of the relatives, and the gold-painted plaster bust of JFK.

Mamá sat on the couch eating oranges. Well, she never really ate them—she chewed them. After she had chewed all the juice out of the orange slice, she'd spit the pulp into a bowl. Later, you'd find bright orange clots of her chewed pulp in the chocolate dirt of the mulch pile. Little molds of Mamá Chayo's mouth feeding the vegetables.

One day, Abelino and I heard a ruckus in the house, women shouting. We rushed in to discover Nina and Fina and Mamá waving their hands and bellowing at the television. Mamá was leading the shouting. She waved one finger at the TV and cried, "Jessie, whatever you do, *don't go in that elevator!*"

Nina, swooning, muttered, "Oh Lord, la Jessie."

Like the character of McGurk in my novel, I had little sense of gardens until I stumbled into theirs.

I shook hands with life in that yard. I met frogs, salamanders, butterflies, birds, worms, lizards, caterpillars, snakes, and mosquito larvae in Abelino's wooden water tanks that I thought were fish—I'd take them home in a jar and set it on the back porch, then be baffled when they'd suddenly be gone. I thought the skeeters were magic creatures.

Their garden was a square acre on a small hilltop. All around the acre were Abelino's houses. At the front, there stood the main house that he had hand-built with his sons. To the west stood another house they built. To the east were two small houses and a strange shed. All of these buildings, rented out to various families, were Abelino's. Unlike my highfalutin father, Abelino left the cannery to enjoy the life of a land baron. Although he was the hardest working man I ever knew, I never really saw him work. Abelino, as long as I knew him, never punched a time card. It seemed to me that he got to play all day.

Across the back of the property was a tall fence that hid a moldering junkyard from view. I never mustered the bravery to go in there. Peeking through the slats at the ruined cars was enough for me. The shattered windshields and the tufts of hair sometimes visible in the glass scared me. And the crane they used to move the cars around looked, to my monster-movie-affected eye, exactly like the giant beasts in *The Black Scorpion*.

At the bottom the hill, swooping from the west to the south, was a brackish tidal wetland. It was a series of estuaries and creeks, salt water sloughs, and mud bogs that separated San Diego from Chula Vista. If you went far enough into the wetlands, you could see the far hill where my aunt worked in a bowling alley. I wasn't down there often, but I went with Abelino several times over the years, harvesting cactus for breakfast.

An old meat-packing plant in the flats occasionally flooded the creeks with offal and blood. When the blood was running, the stench filled the air and followed us all the way up to the junkyard fence. I didn't mind the stink, though. That back fence was where the laundry lines were, and there, the most secret blossoms glowed in the sun. That's

where the astonishing garden of Quela and Fina's under-
wear could be found. It was so brazen. I gawked up at the
wash as it dried, amazed that they'd put it up there for any-
one to see. I touched them, thinking of where they'd been.
And I smelled the sheets, so clean in the sun. And I slipped
my arms into Abelino's vast shirtsleeves. And I watched the
colors as the underpants fluttered: yellow, white, blue, and
color de rosa.

The garden, too, was a kind of miracle, if only for this:
although it occupied one plot of land, it was two completely
different places, depending on which of them led you onto
it. For Abelino, the garden was a place of endless produc-
tivity. It was where he went to raise the food we ate. He had
filled it with sugarcane and quince trees, lettuce and chiles
and *nopales* and avocado trees. He grew corn, cabbage, to-
matoes, onions, squash. Olives. Grapes.

Mamá Chayo, when she took you by the hand and led
you out the back door, took you into a world of fluttering
green. You were suddenly in the midst of butterflies. Hum-
mingbirds chittered in the vines. Mourning doves cooed to
you. She grew carnations, geraniums, roses. Her fences were
covered with honeysuckle.

Abelino harvested peas; Mamá collected sweet pea blos-
soms. (One day, she took me out to show me how sweet pea
blossoms form dog faces, and she showed me if I pinched
the dog's nose just right, its tongue would pop out.) The
one place where their two gardens converged was in their
herb patches. Things that looked like spindly weeds to me

suddenly revealed the flavor of licorice in their hands. Weird little plants growing under the porch were turned into teas that erased stomach pains. Poultices, salves, horrendous drinks came from these patches. Mamá used them to cure coughs, to cure broken bones and varicose veins. Abelino was a master of forcing appalling lengths of tapeworm from people's guts. He delighted in bringing giant mason jars out of the escusado and displaying them to the assembled guests. Inside the jars, writhing feet of worms, and Abelino would laugh and shout, "Oh Gaddamah!"

These herb patches were where they went to find the answers to my TB. Though Mamá was capable of wonders with her teas, she was not in any way cosmic about it. Healing was something she could do, and sometimes she didn't even need herbs. She could be alarmingly direct. To cure *un dolor del oído*, for example, she'd pour pee in your ear.

The rhythms of the garden defined our days. The trees and the birds and the herbs were ready to go by the time the sun was up, and so were we. Abelino was the first out of bed. The sound of his side of their bed squeaking, his wide yawn, the snap of his suspenders in the dark, served as a subtle alarm clock for the rest of us. It was before five o'clock. We'd luxuriate in our beds for a few minutes as he slapped through the house in his wasted leather slippers. He navigated by memory, making his way up the hall, around the dining room table, and into the kitchen. There, the first light of the day would snap on, its gray glow accusing us of being layabouts. He wasn't thinking about us. He

was thinking about his morning constitutional, his break-
fast drink. He pulled down a huge tumbler and cracked two
raw eggs into it. Then he topped off the glass with about
eight ounces of the fierce red wine he made in his backyard
toolshed from his own grapes. He named the wine after
himself. It was almost black, and sweet as Mogen David.
And he'd guzzle it down in one long gulping pull, slurping
the eggs out of the glass and gasping and sighing and belch-
ing and slamming the glass down on the counter. Then he'd
work his fedora onto his head, jack it around on his skull
until it was cocked at the perfect angle, and he'd start to
whistle. It sounded like a stiff wind blowing across the
mouth of a small cave, almost making music, but mostly
making a whooshing sound. To this whooshing, Abelino
added a vibrato that made it sound like he had some melody
in mind when what he really had in mind was joy. He was
blowing the jazz of satisfaction. I never saw him go to
church, but I did see him offer up holy rituals every day
hammering, farting, killing termites, eating fruit, digging
holes, peeling cactus pads, laughing, drinking his wine and
eggs. Abelino was easily the happiest man I ever knew. And
his patch of dirt was the best church I ever prayed in.

After Abelino's morning snort, the women rose. I'd lie in
bed and listen as every quadrant of the house came alive
with the ringing of chamber pots filling with the day's first
cascade. *Triiing!* Mamá. Then *Hrriiing!* and *Prriiing!* Quela
and Fina. And, softly, in the middle distance of the house, a
muffled *Shhh.* Nina.

A parade of women followed, carrying their musically

sloshing pots to the excuse-me. Fina would collect Nina's for her, a ritual of respect. The pots sang out as they walked: *doish,* they said. *Doi-i-ish.* A round of flushing then, and the sound of murmurs and clothes being shaken out in the air, snapping crisply, and silky slidings and the rubbery crack of girdles and bras popping into place, and the billowy sounds of aprons. The day had begun.

Quela and Fina went to the kitchen, and the aromas of dawn began to radiate: coffee, heating lard, on cold days the scent of kerosene in the heater, tortillas. Nina said her rosary. Mamá hustled out the back door to make sure Abelino wasn't about to massacre one of her pansy beds so he could plant more jalapeños.

Mamá Chayo always kissed you on the lips.

Abelino made his own beef jerky. We'd lay the brown strips of smelly steak on wooden drying racks. It looked like a meat laundry hanging in the sun. After the meat had dried into hard planks, we'd attack it with ball-peen hammers, beating it until it splintered. These splinters—except for the ones that accidentally found themselves in my pockets, there to hide until I would act surprised to find them later at snack time—made the tasty dish *machaca.* We ate many unlikely, and some unlovely, things. We loved fried pork skins and dove's breasts that looked like platters of dark noses. Nina and I ate pickled pigs' feet every day, and she seemed to enjoy them even more when I told her I liked to make believe that I was a cannibal and I was eating missionaries. When we weren't hammering on jerky, we were hammering on abalones, trying to soften their meat enough so we could chew it. And when the cane was ready, we'd cut it and spend the day chewing the sugar out of it.

Abelino told me, "Always chop away from yourself when you cut cane. If you don't, you'll chop off a finger."

"Yes sir," I said.

He handed me his machete, and I promptly swung it toward myself, half cutting off my left index finger. I put my hand in my pocket, hoping nobody would notice. When the entire pant leg had turned black with blood, Abelino noticed and bellowed, "Cheezakrytes!" and pulled my hand out of my pocket. The knuckle was white in the cut. He dragged me indoors and delivered me to Mamá Chayo.

I gave them many occasions on which to use their herbs, but that was one of my most spectacular. Mamá didn't even blink. It was the way things worked at West Twentieth. Abelino periodically hacked off a limb, and Mamá tied it back on with three leaves, a root, and a strip of an old skirt.

She'd hand you a tea, or a chalky drink called a *ponche*.

Té de canela.

Té de hierbabuena.

Té de jamaica.

Telimón.

Té de rosas.

I loved collecting the leaves with her. She would bend to the cinnamon, or the jasmine, or the mint, or the lemongrass. Tiny musical frogs lived among the plants. They were yellow-green and emerald and red, bright as candies. They'd jump on her dark arms as she picked, gleam like jewels against her skin for an instant, and vanish again, leaping into invisibility against the green of the garden.

She'd hold up the hem of her apron and I'd fill it—with flowers or grapes, with herbs or peas or fruit. She laughed often. Blue veins wiggled beneath the skin of her gnarled hands. Her hair, hidden in the bun, was obsidian black, and shot through with small lightning bolts of pure white. I always thought of her with short hair, until one day I caught her in the laundry room undoing the braid and letting her hair tumble toward the floor as her startled canaries fluttered in their cages.

She raised canaries, and the laundry room at the back of the house stayed warm all night, so she stacked her breeding cages back there. She made nests for the birds out of tea strainers lined with threads and trimmings from Nina's sewing. Each cage rang all day with such loud bird song that you'd go home and still think you were hearing the birds. Sometimes I'd wake up in our apartment and think for a moment that my parents had bought canaries, so intense was the illusion.

Because the laundry room also contained two huge sinks, the women of the house went back there to wash their hair. All except Nina, whose age had brought her into such a state of grace that she didn't need to wash. All dirt and grime just lifted from her body and was dispersed by the air. Nina's scent was garlic and baby powder.

So one day I was tearing through the house, having escaped one of Abelino's impossible chores, when I stumbled into the laundry room. I could have been seeing a ghost, I was so startled. There she was, Mamá Chayo, bent over before the sink. She had the face of an Aztec queen. And she'd let her hair fall free: it was a waterfall, a veil tumbling over her left shoulder. It covered half of her like a shawl. She stood up and wrestled it over her shoulder, where it fell as far as her bottom. Suddenly, my little Mamá Chayo, in her home-sewn dress and old apron, with her tattered cloth slippers and poochy belly, was tall. She was powerful and fierce, and she couldn't stop smiling. She was young. She was *beautiful*.

Although they were polite to my father, they didn't respect him. I'm not sure they even liked him. No one ever mentioned this, of course. But their unremitting politeness was a soft damnation. They turned their backs on him because they saw him act cruelly toward me one Saturday afternoon when I was five.

We were eating supper. Abelino was at the head of the table, directing the hilarity and chewing with his mouth wide open. Mamá Chayo sat at his right hand, moving tidbits of food onto his plate as he ate, nibbling at her own food, and laughing behind her hand at his outrageous comments. Nina took her traditional spot on the side to his left, her cane hooked over the back of her chair, and her plate mostly empty. Quela and Fina served, and between courses, they sat across from Nina. And I sat with my father at the other end of the table.

Between us, in the middle of the table, was a shifting

astonishment of food. Bowls of *fideo* soup with its toasted noodles. Two plates loaded with steaming fresh tortillas. A serving bowl holding beans floating in their own broth. A bowl of diced *nopalitos*. A plate with raw vegetables on it: lettuce and cabbage with lime juice, red onion, avocado, carrots, chiles. Bowls of salsa. Bowls of salt, for Abelino didn't use salt shakers; we'd take a pinch and scatter it over our food like seeds. Rice. And the meat. Coffee, water, tea, milk. And after, impossibly, dessert. A glass of *vino*.

Everything was going well, too: we were all laughing, and Quela was close enough so I could touch her feet with mine, and my father was funny, lighting up the table with his jokes, when I reached for the milk. Knocked it over. Milk cascaded everywhere.

My father had quick reflexes. Before anyone could say a word, he was out of his seat, roaring my name. He grabbed my ankle and hoisted me into the air upside down and struck me in the face. And they, upside down, staring at me with their mouths open—silent.

They never fed him again. And they took to preparing elaborate suppers for my mother, which they'd ask him to deliver to her when he took me home. Those meals, balanced on my lap, would radiate heat into my belly as we drove. They felt like Mamá Chayo was burning into me, like she could fill my insides with warmth and stay there forever, keeping something deep in me alive just in case the cold came. Some comfort between my belly and my spine, in case the snow ever caught me unprepared.

So it was all about love, starting with love for each other.

Every night, when Abelino had come in from his point-lessly busy days, and after their nightly feast, he'd cruise over to the couch and recline. He'd pull out his dentures, spit a load into the spittoon, then settle in to enjoy a full evening of shouting insults at the television. Mamá Chayo, having supervised the cooking, would relinquish the cleanup to the twins. She'd collect her latest crocheting project and take her traditional spot at the other end of the couch, where she'd chuckle at his outbursts. Nina, if she was awake, would say from her corner, "Oh boy, Compadre, you're really on tonight!" But mostly, she'd snore. When she started, Abelino would nudge Mamá and point at Nina and laugh.

I'd watch then for the special love gesture. I almost quivered with anticipation. Some nights it took forever. On other nights it happened right away. But it always happened.

I wonder now if they each knew that the gesture was going to happen. And maybe, just maybe, they held back, sort of stalled, to build anticipation, like saving that toffee crunch in the chocolate box until last. Maybe, even though they were my godparents, my elders, maybe this was a sensual delight for them. They had a lot of kids: they were sexy. They were in their sixties and their seventies, and they were sexy.

So maybe it was one of those sexually as well as emotionally satisfying gestures. Like when someone you love takes your elbow in a crowd. Like when you hold hands. Or when, late in the night, you reach out your hand and catch the cup of the hipbone of your partner—just to feel the warmth, the life there. Or when somebody absent-mindedly runs her fingers through your hair, like a comb, like your fairy godmother's fingertips were on your scalp, or your mom's, and it makes you want to cry and it makes you want to go to sleep. A palm against your cheek.

I'd watch for it, and sooner or later, Abelino's battered old slippers would come off, and he'd ease his legs up on the couch, and his feet would start to creep. His thin black socks would bunch around his rocky ankles, making a pouch at his toes. And those feet, first one, then the other, would move toward her like cats sniffing around the couch pillows. The feet wandered down the couch, found her leg as if by accident, then moved up into her lap. His smelly toes would push her crochet needles aside. And she'd turn and put her work in a bowl with a small tinkle, then turn off the lamp, and turn to watch TV, the lenses of her glasses glowing blue with reflected light, like she was shooting love beams out of her eyes. Then, never looking at his feet, she'd put her hands on them. She wouldn't massage them, she'd *touch* them. Hold them. Cup them. Feel his arches and toes. Run her palms up and down them. It was the most extraordinary thing, this foot fondling. And you could see his delighted toes in there, wiggling around in his socks. Nestled in her dear lap. Bunching up her skirt.

Now, imagine the darkest day of our lives, when she died.

It was sudden—a stroke as she stood beside their bed, on the side she'd slept on for fifty years, the side she had risen on every morning to follow him into the day. She fell to the floor beside her chamber pot, where they found her. Gone.

And the funeral, which is where this is all heading. I want you at the funeral. Her children, her nieces and nephews, her grandchildren, her acolytes and me. Devastated. And Abelino, this hard old man, fierce, solitary. He spent the whole funeral attending to the mourners, patting my mother on the back, holding up the ones who went to the open coffin and collapsed. He wore a suit that looked like he'd owned it since 1948.

At this funeral, I saw Abelino's ultimate gesture of love. It wasn't for me to see, but like Mamá Chayo's hair, it was a secret I was lucky enough to glimpse. And it has stayed with me all these years, Abelino's mute poem. His mute symphony.

Right at the end, after all the many mourners had passed by, after my father had gone out to hide in his car, right before they closed the box forever and carried it to the hearse, Abelino stepped up to her. He didn't weep. He stood silently, gazing down at his one love, his one true destined love, the companion of more than a lifetime, and he studied her face. Then, with no emotion showing on his face, he reached into the coffin and put his palm against her cheek. His big, iron, calloused worker's hand. It trembled slightly, and it landed on her flesh as delicately as one of her butterflies. Just a second, no more. But all the love in the world was there, in his palm. All the love in the universe, and all the tenderness, and all the grief, and all the beauty collected there in his hand and lay against her lovely cheek.

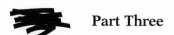 **Part Three**

Leaving Shelltown

White birds over the grey river.
Scarlet flowers on the green hills.
I watch the Spring go by and wonder
if I shall ever return home.

Tu Fu

I pull into Johnson's Corner Truck Stop, off I-25, heading north on the high plains of Colorado. To my left, the cracked spine of the Rockies is massively visible, pale violet between me and my past. Lately, I've been thinking about Logan Heights—what the *pachucos* used to call "Shelltown"—National Avenue, and the knives and the shotguns and the glass. I have driven over the Continental Divide, I have driven up and down the Front Range, climbed the Flatirons, climbed out of the Grand Canyon, swum in Emerald Pool high up in Zion. But Shelltown doesn't go away. Thomas Wolfe said, "You can't go home again." I'd like to add: sometimes you can't escape from home, no matter how far you go.

Inside Johnson's, all the booths have phones; truckers sit around me in their gimme caps. Graffiti in the toilet: CRAZY COYOTES/TEXAS. The rubber machines offer "Love Paks" for seventy-five cents. Having a prime rib sandwich special. Destination: Laramie, Wyoming. Songs on the jukebox include:

"Ace in the Hole" by George Strait

"Timber I'm Falling in Love" by Patty Loveless

and

"There's a Tear in My Beer" by Hank Williams Jr.

All heads turn when a baby-blue '50 Chevy lowrider pulls through the lot, the cowboys and me suddenly transformed into homeboys. I wonder what these red-faced straw hats would do if a vato walked in right now, khakis pulled up high, Pendleton buttoned at the throat, maybe a red bandana flat on his forehead, surgically slicing off the top curve of his eyebrows. I can hear them now, muttering *Gaw-Damn Sioux!*

Mexicans out here lie low. I know a Chicana poet who teaches at the University of Colorado, and every semester or so, some genius in a truck calls her a "greaser" or an "Injun." A verbal drive-by shooting. It's funny: I never heard an anti-Mexican comment in Shelltown. For whatever bad things I could say about Logan, that is the best. When I moved to Clairemont in fifth grade, I was suddenly being called the following: *beaner, taco-bender, pepper-belly, spic.* My father had warned me about *greaser* and *wetback*. But these new words were spectacular and vivid. I couldn't figure out what we had done to make them so mad at us.

The meat in my sandwich is a huge gray slab. I'm wearing black jeans and cowboy boots. Got $200. . . well $180. Got a full tank of gas. . . well half a tank. Bought a Johnson's Corner postcard for religious vision and inspiration:

Trucker's Prayer

Let me live my life
with fast trucks and beautiful women,
and when I die, I want them to tan
this old hide of mine,
and make it into a ladies driving seat,
so that I'll be between the two things I like best.
Fast trucks and beautiful women.

Amen.

I drive north.

Cache La Poudre River.

I cross into Wyoming the back way, up Highway 287, the former stagecoach route. Ruined stage stations lurk in the hollows, suspicious ghosts at the busted windows, fingering their six-guns. A lone buffalo stands broadside to the road. His chin beard makes him look like a *veterano.* He watches me go by. I hear him say, *"Qué onda, Homes?"*

Laramie, Wyoming. State bird: meadowlark.

My tent takes only about five and a half minutes to put up. I pitch it in the middle of a wide grass field. My little house on the micro-prairie. Distant mountains; clouds come up from the plains. Quiet blackbirds patrol the grass. Big trucks on I-80 rumble vaguely behind. My Jeep looks noble and jaunty against a fractured sky.

Found: one stainless steel fork in the grass. Says "New York State" on the handle. Some fresh-sprung jailbird stole his chili spoon from the mess-line. I police the area like the blackbirds, solemnly looking for bugs.

Unbelievable light. The sun slants close to the ground and pure heartbreak light floods all across the landscape, pushing my shadow like a log on a wave. Storm clouds in the distance start as a blue-gray smear near the earth and knot and tumble and rise and grow to massive bright-white fists twelve miles high.

I'm hunched in my tent like a woodchuck.

Lone supper: really gnarly hash on French roll, some cheese, Triscuits. Dates, bananas, milk.

Kind of like eating an Alpo sandwich.

Other lonely guys scattered around the field eat their suppers, too, look up at the clouds, the far peaks, the high plains. Rain on the horizon as vague between the clouds and land as smoke. The sun is so low behind me now that the hurrying shadows of the semis stretch across a mile or so and hit the tent wall. Gray flashes. The white face of the tent has developed an eyelid and it is blinking. Squads of stealthy bears leap out of the grass.

One Logan Heights event always comes back to me. I often see it in my mind at quiet moments. It's funny, I think.

3935 National Avenue, maybe 1963 or '64. My father was

no doubt bowling. (He worked at the Hillcrest Bowl—gone now, I've noticed. Its murals of Rip Van Winkle and bowling trolls lost forever to yet another San Die Go mini-mall, not far from where our town fathers bulldozed that graveyard to make a devil's park.) My mom and I were in the apartment, barricaded by her insane fear of black people.

It was obvious to me, even at a young age, that she caused the problems in the first place. Just like the knuckleheads in Clairemont who would later call *my people* "greasers," my mother thought nothing of using the "N" word, a word I dread to this day. She explained that "we don't mean anything when we call them that, honey—it's just their name." So our nights were spent in a darkened apartment, all doors and windows locked, with my mother no doubt imagining waves of invaders desperate to get in at us and our turtle and our tin TV trays.

That night, I was awakened by a ruckus across the lawn. The next building down was having a house party—black voices laughing to the terrific funque of James Brown: *Please, Please, Please!* The last thing I remember hearing before I fell asleep was the melodic voice of the large woman I had never been allowed to meet. I thought it was her yelling when I awoke.

It was not. It was a man screaming in a perfect falsetto. He was wailing like the Four Tops. Mother was at the window. "Don't look," she said. I looked. Yow!

He was running around naked. Buck—or "butt" as the homeys used to say—naked. I think he was the first man I had ever seen naked, except for my father. He was certainly the first black man I had seen naked. He was skinny and periodically appeared in washes of light as he paraded around the lawn, declaiming. Oh, and he was waving a long twelve-gauge shotgun right at the pleasant large woman who stood on the porch saying "baby" and "fool." The party-goers were ducking to the floor as he aimed at the house.

Police cars flashed hysterically on National Avenue. Cops crept up all around him, speaking sweetly. He yelled at them, too. I remember this so vividly because it could never happen today. The cops moved in on him, stood with him, reasoned with him, took the gun from him, then everyone laughed.

This pissed off the large woman on the porch, who lit into the cops and him. In the following excitement, as they tried to keep the shotgun from her, tried to keep her from him, he slipped away. The next thing any of us knew, one of the cop cars took off—our hero at the wheel. He'd done a quick bit of nude sidewalk auto shopping. All the other cops lit out after him.

The party-goers laughed for about an hour.

I went back to bed.

The thinnest nail clipping of a moon is up. Electric lights look cold and alien in the near distance. Local kids actually ride brakes on the dirt country road while I'm thinking it's the end of the world.

Tents have sprung up around me. Bikers build a small compound of four tents, massive Harleys circled against the Pawnee—or the cavalry. A guy with a swollen lens before his face stands and films the weird western horizon.

And now, on Interstate 80, the big rigs fly through amber washes of electric lightning. It looks like they're plastic toys. Like there's a bulb inside each truck making it glow. Then they're past the lights, and they blink out. Turn black against the sky. Phantom boxes, damned to an eternal rush everywhere in this huge America.

There goes one now.

Really cold now. No doubt the Big Alone drops the temp another five degrees. I get in, zip shut the tent, pull on a long-sleeved T-shirt. Put on my wife's socks for comfort. Into the bag. Miss her.

It's only after a little while that I start crying.

Late enough for pitch blackness. I unzip my tent flap and cautiously peek out. The moon is so low, so lurid in its color, and so distorted by the atmosphere, that I mistake it for a neon sign.

Morning.

The inside of the tent is completely coated with condensation. I have breathed a small rainstorm.

Radio suddenly delivers horrible news: It's only 6:51 A.M.

Driving through the rolling grasslands. Groups of cows and horses bunch together and stare out upon the morning. Also a little flock of rust-red tractors. Look like they're grazing.

I've been listening to an AM station. They have a show called "The Trading Post," in which various Wyomingians call in to sell stuff. I find their pithy cowboy accents oddly comforting in the middle of the big empty range. Due to the relentless road racket of the Jeep, however, their words can barely be understood. Strange new phrases and surreal sentences pop out of my radio: "A zubukon mastiff—hee-hee-haw!—fifteen fifty-six."

Now, the Jeep hisses and spits its entire radiator load all over the blacktop. I pour in fresh water and head out—six miles to the next gas station. Steaming like a *zubukon mastiff*.

I always loved gas stations. Machines roar all through my San Diego memories: my old man, working in the back end of the Hillcrest Bowl among those amazing Brunswick pin tenders, reading moldy nudie mags like *Nugget* and *Pix* and *Knight*. And there I was, scampering over the open guts of the machines on catwalks, shooting SMERSH and KAOS agents off the rafters to screaming bone-shearing deaths inside the gears: their heads would routinely be delivered back to the stunned bowlers in place of bowling balls. And we hung out at Sherbet's Shell (a fake name, and anyway, it's gone now too.) Sherbet was a cowpoke-looking dude who belonged eternally at Johnson's Corner. He'd cheerfully repair the damage the old man did to our new Comet on our jaunts into Tijuana.

I didn't notice that we hung out at Sherbet's because my dad and Mrs. Sherbet were in love. She was a cotton-eyed-Joe cowgirl who seemed to think an organ-playing bowling-shoe attendant was just the neatest thing. She showed up at my house one morning when my mom was at work. "What are you doing here?" she said. "I live here," I said and shut the door.

Sherbet died of cancer, whittled down to seventy innocent pounds. He never knew, but she could not forget. I never saw her again.

Boil over.

I clang and belch into the dirt back lot of Elk Mountain Texaco station. It's like Jim Bridger's wilderness outpost, smack in the middle of nothing much. A fellow in an orange jumpsuit comes out and looks at it. Steam rising.

"It's a warm one," he says.

"Sure is," I drawl. Real he-man stuff happening.

"Could be the thermostat."

"Gauge says normal. Stays right in the middle."

"Gauge says normal, huh?"

"Middle. Little *less* than middle."

He looks.

"Could be the pump. Could be the cap. Could be the thermostat's stuck."

I have no idea what he's talking about.

"Hunh," I say in manly appreciation.

"Let's let her cool down."

He goes back inside.

A second car guru in an orange jumpsuit comes out for a look. We bend into the open mouth of the Jeep, and he asks pertinent questions.

"It's gonna have to cool down a little bit," he says. "But I guess *he* already told you that."

He goes back inside.

Guy comes back out. Says, "This might still be pretty God-damned close to hot!"

Then he goes back inside.

His jumpsuit, in white thread, says JIM.

Several dead cars crouch in the grass. A giant tow-truck beside me mutters to itself: "Ten-four. . .Edwards. First name Ralph W." The back of the tow-truck has a plaque that says HOLMES 750, whatever that means. Jim returneth.

"It's the thermostat," he says.

It has malfunctioned, causing the water to fail to circulate.

"Got to see if I got a new one," he says. "This God-damned thing's shot! If I don't, you got to go on down the road without one and see if you can find you one."

He goes back inside.

He comes back out.

"Got one," he says.

Then we go into a head-gasket panic. The radiator keeps boiling over. "If it's the gasket," Orange Jim tells me, "then you're up the crick."

I engage in brisk dialogue with God.

"God-damned head gasket, you could have cooked the God-damned thing," Jim notes.

He goes back inside.

He comes back out.

"Done," he says.

I get ready to leave. One of the mechanics comes out and proclaims: "Aw, muckerfutch!"

Which is exactly how I feel.

Driving out among the prairies, I think: *This ain't Clairemont Drive!*

At strange, abandoned Fort Fred Steele.

In a word, desolate. The interpretive center is abandoned. Wind whistles. Nobody home.

Ruins. Chimneys, stark and tall, like photographs of abandoned concentration camps. I think of my mother with the Red Cross, tagging after Patton as he busted open the doors of Buchenwald. Everybody dead and gone: Patton, the victims, the good soldiers of Fort Steele, my mother. Dust under the sun. It looks exactly like my memories.

These boys at Fort Steele were truly at the end of the line.

Now, the entire fort belongs to eerie birds, crickets, and me. The only sound is the wind, the animals, and furious-sounding freight trains going by.

Collapsing cabins and stables, vast rubble-pebbled grass and empty foundations. I climb down into an underground storeroom. Dirt steps uncertain, old door warped and angled into the earth. Splintery shelves set into the dirt walls. Pack-rat droppings like scattered punctuation in the corners.

On the ground: triangles of busted porcelain, old bottles, nails, ancient flattened food tins, bits of windows. A dead falcon lies by the foundation of the enlisted men's barracks. Headless. A safe lies tipped on its back, door ripped off. Thin scum of rusty rainwater inside and a chemical-leaking Polaroid half-developed: a demon's eye view of the smoke-stacks, colors sunburned and melted.

Ghosts! I keep expecting to hear boot heels or a horse.

Across the prairie grass parade ground, an old white schoolhouse still stands.

It is near the edge of a small bluff, and I can imagine the children of a hundred years sitting inside, gazing out the windows, dreaming of buffalo and Cheyenne warriors.

Inside the old schoolhouse, graffiti:

———

Went to school here
in 1912 was
here in 1975

      James Spyer

———

went to school here
to 1924   JAS RAWLINS

———

TM
-N-
D.A.

FEB
5
1958

_____

Devil Place Call 1-800-666-EVIL

_____

Lee Sandoval
started kinter garden Here
        1927
Married Marina
Best days of my life

_____

Lived across tracks in 1959
was here 6-9-81
                    James Sanchez

_____

I was here come and find me bitch!

_____

This place is not for you so get the fuck out. I was here
first so this is my fucken place stay away MP

"This is my fuckin' neighborhood," Jerome used to say.
"I'll fuckin' run you out, white child."

We were all terrified of Jerome, the black kids and me
both. But in his way, he loved his own. Certainly, Jerome's
wrath was directed most deliberately at us—the Mexicans
and whites and pinays (Filipinos).

He had a short leg. He wore a thick-soled shoe. He
thumped and strained around the 'hood, swinging his leg

wide. Sometimes he'd take a swipe at me as he went by. Once, a gaggle of his homeboys brass-knuckled me in the kidneys as I walked by them. I was with my mother, and I walked on tiptoes, biting back on the pain until they were well past. I'd show them I could take it. But I also knew that if my mother noticed, she'd start trouble, and I was more afraid of that than of the pain.

One day, coming home from school, I saw a small black kitten caught in the middle of National Avenue. It had a ribbon around its neck with a small bell that tinkled as it flinched away from the cars and meowed.

I rescued it.

My mother let it sleep with me that night. The next morning, we put it out. She said, "If it still comes back after school, you can keep it."

But after school, it was gone.

I waited and waited. Finally I asked some kids going by, "Have you seen a kitten?"

One of the girls said, "You mean a little black one? Got a bell?"

"Yeah!"

"Jerome kilt it. Smashed its head with his shoe. He left it stickin' to the wall of the laundry room."

Later, the homeys would bury another cat in wet cement.

One swing through the cemetery before I go. It's an abandoned, worn-down, Wild West boneyard on a bluff above the river. Windswept. I want to pay my respects. There's a placard with names and dates of death of each person in each numbered grave. (Headstones long gone now.) I decide to find someone who died near this date, figuring no one had been along to mourn the anniversary of their passing for a hundred years.

Clara Kesner died August 3, 1871. She was buried at position twenty-one. She was the daughter of Sergeant Kesner, Second U.S. Cavalry. When the troops pulled out, they dug young Clara up and mounted her on a train. Her casket was borne away to a national cemetery far away—there, I hope, to lie eventually beside her father. I count off the sinking plots and find twenty-one. I kneel for a minute and wish her well. I am startled at the strength of my feelings.

I leave her the blossoms of weeds, tucked onto the spot by rocks.

Crossed the Continental Divide—twice. I don't know how I managed that. TIRED. Many gas and rest stops. Everybody gets out of cars and walks the same way, like we've each got an emery board tucked between our butt cheeks. I reward Wyoming with a little more of my urine.

I keep scanning for flying saucers. So far I've only sighted old fat guys in overalls.

Pulled into an "eighteen-wheeler restaurant." About to eat a happy chef's salad, happy corn bread, and a happy cup of coffee. Truckers again. Phones at all the tables. Quoth the Noble Knights of the Road:

"When the hell is the God-damned dog going in!"

"I bet Terry's been beatin' her gums."

One guy enthuses:

"All I need's a coffee cup and an ashtray and I'm all set!"

Clouds put down spider legs of lightning and mince along the peaks.

Green River.

Blacks Fork River.

We're all restless out here. Americans hurrying away. That seems the quintessential American direction: away. Maybe that's why I couldn't stay in San Diego anymore. There was no place left to run.

Here's how I got out of Shelltown. Physically at least.

After school, 1965: spring. Wearing my idiotic St. Jude's Academy uniform. My bright red sweater calling vatos and homeboys from miles around to come kick my ass. I had a crew cut because I thought it made me sound like James Bond in the barber shop. "What'll it be, kid," the old fart would say. "Crew cut," I'd say, imagining I was puffing on a cigarette. All the stinky men in there would laugh, and the barber would turn to my old man and say, "Get a load of this kid." And, along with my uniform, I had my brown satchel full of books and pencils. You could hear the 'hood telegraph calling: *Here comes a geek!*

The cat was old—eighteen, maybe even twenty. He was light brown, had a close-cropped do, and stank of burned hemp, though I was too little really to know what weed smelled like. And I was thrilled. We walked down the street chatting away like friends.

Up ahead, two good St. Jude's girls in *their* uniforms.

"Look at that," he said.

"Yeah."

"You like girls?"

"Yeah!"

"You really like girls?"

"Sure!"

He yelled: "Hey, girls! This boy say he want to get into your pussies!"

"I didn't say that!" I said.

"You say I'm lying?" he said, then he punched me in the mouth. I covered up. He landed a couple to my forearms, then started in on my ears and the back of my head. I panicked and swung my satchel into his face. The whole world stopped. Freeze-frame. Then the satchel slowly came off his lips in rebound, and his eyes locked on mine. No sound as the lips work, spitting words I can no longer hear. And he reaches into his back pocket, things speeding back up to normal, and he yanks a switchblade out and he hits the button and the blade flies up, out, bright, sharp. And he swings.

I wasted no time. I was gone. I imagine a cloud of cartoon dust in my wake, as if I were the Roadrunner and this maniac were Wile E. Coyote.

I was running hard, and he was gaining, and I swear I heard the blade fly past my ear as he swung it, yelling, "I'mo kill you!" over and over. I have dreaded running and jogging ever since then. But I won that race, beating it into Mr. Everrett's Antiques. (Gone now, too, like all the rest.) And I was screaming, "He's killing me!" Mr. Everrett, a gruff old sport who raised pugs, lived in a house in back. He came out of the back room and said, "Who's killing you?" That was when Wile E. Coyote burst in, waving his knife. Mr. Everrett magically reversed his age about thirty-five years and jumped to a counter and grabbed an antique butcher knife. I was between the two blade points, gawking up at their twisted faces.

"Boy hit me, I'mo kill him."

"You're not killing anybody. Now get out of here."

"I'mo cut him."

"Big Man," Mr. Everrett taunted. "You're such a big man to chase little boys!"

There was no phone—something pretty common on National Avenue in those days. Wile E. went outside, but laid siege, hovering around the front door for a half hour. Mr. Everrett finally ran out as a police car passed, and Wile E. vanished, never to be seen again. I was afraid every day for a while, certain he would grab me on my way to school.

But the story didn't end just there. It should have, but it didn't. What happened was that Wile E.'s siege had made me almost an hour late to my baby-sitter's. She did not believe me when I told her what had happened. And there was no way to call Mr. Everrett.

She told my parents, who also thought I was lying. There was a good chance I had stayed after school in one of *their* houses. Soon, there would be children bearing the "N" word all over our house. And worse, I had lied.

So my father made me take off my pants, and he whipped me with his belt. He was sad about it, of course, but he was teaching me to tell the truth. Only, the next day, Mr. Everrett checked to see how I was, and they realized their mistake.

Apparently, the whipping finally made them leave Shelltown.

Sign:
THE CROSS IS BARE
THE TOMB IS EMPTY
JESUS LIVES !

Onto Uinta County, Highway 295. Dirt. To Hole in the Wall. I'm in Butch Cassidy Country; Sundance, the Wild Bunch, Kid Curry (that outlaw with the rock-'n'-roll name), they all rode through here. I've got the joyous glow of gunfighter ghosts in the Jeep with me. Butch, looking a little bony today, wears his dopey Boston bowler hat.

Two cows happily munch beside the track as I drive in and stop to watch. I get out and walk over near them and say, "Hi cows."

Hey! They're bulls! Run away!

On up the track a ways, driving in four-wheel drive through slick mud. I come upon two fellows standing in the mud. One with a cowboy hat. The other with long black hair, apparently an Indian. They've been pulling a trailer with a Blazer, and they've got the trailer stuck. So they unhook it and immediately bury the Blazer up to its rocker panels. Thomas McGuane described this very scene in one of his novels: "These men seemed to feel their pickup owed them an explanation."

I pull up behind the trailer. For some reason, I suddenly affect a western twang. Utterly phony good ol' boy speak. Maybe I'm channeling Kid Curry. "Yuh git stuck?" I bellow.

"Yep! Never seen it this way!"

"*Huh!*"

"You goin' all the way up?"

"Not now I'm not!"

"Too bad."

"Jes' pokin' around."

"How 'bout that!"

"Guesst I'll go poke someplace else!"

"Don't get off that gravel!" he advises.

The Indian man flashes me a peace sign.

Welcome to Utah. Flocks of sheep file across the hills. I have been driving and driving and driving and driving. Driving, driving, driving, driving, and driving. In the far distance, lightning strikes set a tree afire. I watch it burn, an angry wavering amber-yellow-red point. Then it flickers out. Jimi Hendrix playing as I sink into psychedelic Flaming Gorge.

Sheep Creek Canyon. Not another humanoid in sight. Three overgrown graves in an overgrown corral up a rise to the right of the road. Cleophas J. Dowd, 1857–1897. Homesteaded here from 1885 till his death. He must have been feeling testy in '97, because he was killed by his partner,

Charles Reaser, in "self defense." Religious nut, visionary, gunman, crank, rancher, swindler—ol' Dowd's buried in his beloved canyon with two of his kids. I don't know if I'd have liked Cleophas in life, but I'm happy for him in death. Not a bad spot at all for your ghost to wander. You could say Cleophas J. Dowd homesteaded Sheep Creek Canyon for eternity.

A delightful and surreal little ridge line trail meanders up from Mr. Dowd's grave. I leave him and hike up a short way and dig the sounds of animals, water, the coolness, the green and red soil. The walls have, in places, the same outré colors as Bryce Canyon. I'm so busy gawking at the cliffs that I almost plow into an antelope.

I park at the mouth of the canyon, beside Navajo cliffs, and think about the basic worthiness of living, what Jonathan Edwards would have called "beauty" and "sweetness." God in the details, like Jonathan saw the divine in a lightning storm or a spider. Out in the aloneness and the silvery collapsing homesteaders' shacks visible in the near distance all along the highway, I think about Jerome, and Mr. Jones, the only man who could comfort me after Jerome had killed my kitten.

Mr. Jones was a minister who lived across the dirt alley. He had the purest black skin I ever saw, a beautiful shade of obsidian, and startlingly white hair. He always wore a suit. Once, when I had to go into his house because I had thrown a toy into his backyard, I was astonished to find him wearing a hair net.

I was crying in the dirt. Mr. Jones came along the fence and peered in at me. He was carrying his Bible. "Boy," he said. "What are you crying about?"

I was sure only Mr. Jones could understand what had happened, so I ran to him, grabbed him over the fence, and wailed, "Jerome killed my little cat!"

Mr. Jones just stood there quietly and patted me until I stopped crying. Then he said, "Wait here for me."

He came back from his house with a small silver box. It had "1898" etched on it. He handed it to me.

"It was my wife's," he said. She had died before I was born. "Open it."

Inside, an old rosary.

"They gave that to her when she was a little girl," he said. "And she gave it to me when she died. Now you take it."

I stood there with the box in my hands and stared up at him. I knew that something huge was happening, but I couldn't know what. He said: "You remember Mr. Jones when you get sad. You keep this with you and remember this day. And I want you to remember that black men are men, not niggers."

He put his hand on my head, and he went home.

Today, walking along beside Sheep Creek, I happened to come across a perfect place to stop, a flat pale rock. On this rock, a fat black ant. It gave me pleasure to step beside her, my foot 1,000 times her size, and be gone. The ant, pausing in her motions, thought—with whatever micro-electric sparks ants use for thought—*what was that?* Then each of us went about our business, unharmed. (Though she might have had a religious conversion. She might have rushed back to the nest, squirting the chemical message to her mates: "I saw God! It sat beside me upon the rock then flew into the sky!")

Flaming Gorge, Utah: Sleeping above the drowned ghost of Linwood, near the shore of Linwood Bay.

Wind and lightning and rain. Trash from farms swirls like leaves. A paper sign floats onto my windshield and glues itself there. Innocent children's scrawls: *BEWARE OF DOG German Shepeard don't touch this stuff or well be in trable.*

Er, I hope it's children's scrawls.

What a night.

The storm kicks in heavily as the sun drops, rain pelting and thunder roaring. And me camped under a cottonwood, watching lightning hit trees a few miles away. Lightning—tree. This particular cottonwood being the tallest thing on the small range where I'm camped. Tree—lightning. Lightning + tree = fried me. I grab my little tent and wrestle the entire thing across the flooding field to a relatively dry spot, then I run back, barefoot, in my underwear, and drive the Jeep to the tent. I have formulated some inane scientific theory that the Jeep is grounded, being on rubber tires, and will somehow keep lightning from finding me out, nestled like a hedgehog in the short grass.

There is a tent beside mine, and a man inside sounds like a sleeping bear. Thunder rumbles, and he responds with an aerosol event of his own: *bweeeeet!*

Then, I can't sleep. The rain on the nylon makes a loud plastic racket. It snaps and pops so loudly that I imagine I'm caught in the yolk of a giant sunny-side-up egg cooking on God's griddle.

The rain slacks off.

Still can't sleep.

I lie there listening to the guy next door. *Ronk!* he announces. *R-r-o-o-nk!* That's when the phantom horses strike.

First, all the dogs in the area start to bark. You can hear them on distant ranches, and outside medium-distance trailers, and behind close-by fences. Then I hear a muted clanging and tinkling, like cowbells or sleigh bells. I hear the bells cross the field, moving between the other scattered tents. I look outside but see nothing. The dogs are just sick about it, too.

Once the bells die down, neighing can be heard fifty yards to my right. It's that unmistakable horse sound. The drum of pounding hooves follows. Gallump-gallump past me in the dark. Apparently, nobody else hears it: no heads poke out of neighboring tents. I dash back and forth, trying to see the horses. Darkness. Nothing.

The galloping runs back and forth, back and forth, until finally it vanishes as quickly as it began. Not another sound. The dogs die down in fits and starts, until there's nothing but crickets and *Ronk!* echoing across the field.

Some time later I drift off. I don't know what weird dreams the horses inspire, but I wake up and jerk out of my sleeping bag uttering a mysterious name: Elmer Gatch!

Flaming Gorge Dam, Utah.

I follow a family with a miniature poodle onto the roadway atop the dam. A very pleasant ranger in blue with pleasant and profuse blond hair and a very pleasant voice appears. She points out various fascinating things to us and the poodle, including the cascades of water that seep around the edges of the dam wall and come tearing out through the mountainsides. I angle in for a look at her name tag. Our guide: Clare D. Clare has an especially pleasant form, and I follow it loyally all over the dam. And I love? Her voice? That ends each sentence? About the dam? In a question?

Also, Clare caught a thirty-pound trout in the gorge at 4:30 this very morning. I swoon. Love, blind love.

"Our record catch at Flaming Gorge," Fair Clare croons, "was 51.8 pounds!"

Then Clare terrorizes me by leading us into the bowels of the dam in an elevator. I stand at the bottom, watching happy trout loaf around in the whirls of water from the overflow, dreadfully aware that the world's tallest tidal wave rises right behind me, frozen by a thin membrane of cement.

I fall on the Hiway 64 Motel.

Lula Long checks me in.

The motel office is set up behind a counter in her dining

room. In the living room, out of sight around a partition, somebody watches Andy of Mayberry. Andy's saying, "Well he's not a snoop or a foreign spy." *I'm not*, I agree. The woman watching the TV laughs.

Lula looks at me and says, "God."

She's thin as a breeze, gray hair in a neat little do. She wears a filmy blouse and a housecoat. Ashtrays overflowing with cigarette butts can be seen on the counter and on the dining-room table. A clear air hose runs to Lula's nose. She drags a small air unit with her as she moves, carefully laying her hands on things, as if they were hot. She has a dark scar on her throat.

She takes a very long time filling out the forms.

"It takes me forever," she says.

"Don't worry about it."

All my feelings go out and around Lula Long.

I cannot imagine her days.

Vegetating in my room. Happy to be on a bed. Dully staring at the various boyz of *Young Guns* running around going "Pow! Pow!" on the TV. My legs are knobby with bug bites. From ankles to kneecaps, I'm covered in red bumps. My legs are like the handles of some newfangled, heavy-duty "shur-grip" screwdrivers.

On TV, Jon Bon Jovi sings, "I'm going out in a blaze of glory." While I'm going out in a blaze of hemorrhoids.

If only we could rob a bank. If only we could wield a six-gun and make it all better. I would ride into my past and shoot the daylights out of everything, grab everybody and gallop into the sunset. But Shelltown eats its young. It eats its old, too. Man, you can't shoot a ghost.

I'd lay odds I'm the first National Avenue boy to hike Sheep Creek Canyon. Jerome's dead as my cat; Wile E. Coyote is rubble at the base of the street. My dad's dead. Mr. Everrett's dead. My baby-sitter's dead. San Diego's dead: I go home and find hilltops scraped off by some idiot in a tractor and pushed into the canyons. Clairemont's surrounded by a fungus of yuppie condos, clattering beehives just waiting for that big fire to smear them off the hillsides. Rattlesnakes, owls, foxes, coyotes, scorpions, alligator lizards cram into little ravines behind Clairemont High School. Building up to their revenge.

And my mother. She was so American she fled: from New York to World War II; from Buchenwald to San Francisco; from Sausalito to Mexico and my father; from my father to loneliness; from Tijuana to Shelltown; from Shelltown to Clairemont. But she couldn't shake Shelltown out of herself. It ate her up from within. Poverty had grabbed all of us and housed itself in our hearts. Poverty was home. She stayed in her house alone, poor in spirit, and couldn't get up the coins to pay for another escape. There is no way to pay for the things you have compromised.

In April of 1990 she went to bed and never woke up. She lay there almost a week. Neighbors broke in and found her on her side, blankets pulled to her chin. Beside her in the bed, a Bible and a cookbook. I was so broke I had to borrow money to cremate her. I returned to the land of the dead to recover her body. After I fed her ashes to the ocean, I began to run.

Saturday.

Woke up at eight after strange dreams. In one, a little girl was making camp with me, but I don't know who she was. In another, a child kept hugging me and saying, "My best buddy." In the last, I was watching a basketball game. My father turned to me and asked, "Is this a national sport?"

Lula Long says, "Come back and see me."

She's smoking a cigarette. Smoke curls out her nostrils and rolls over her air hose like a small wave. I don't know how to tell her what I have to tell her.

The ghosts and I pile into the Jeep. The kitten's on the dash. My father's beside me looking at the map. My mother sits uncomfortably beside Jerome. Cleophas J. Dowd is skinnier than all of them. I hope Mr. Jones is still alive somewhere touching some little boy on top of his head.

I drive out of town and look down upon the White River, on one of the many spots where the Escalante expedition crossed, on September 9, 1776. They called it the San Clemente. Father Escalante and his men wandered in these unforgiving hills and canyons trying to find a passage west from Santa Fe. Hoping somehow to find a highway to California. I sit here staring at their bewildering landscape, can feel them wondering what to do now. Do they cross the San Clemente again? Do they turn back? Can they go home and forget their strange sojourn?

The engine rumbles eagerly.

I don't know where I'm going.

source acknowledgments

The following poems are reprinted with permission:

"Do Not Be Ashamed." © Wendell Berry. *Collected Poems: 1957–1982* (San Francisco: North Point Press, 1985).

"Another Spring," by Tu Fu, from *One Hundred Poems from the Chinese,* edited by Kenneth Rexroth (New York: New Directions, 1971).

Portions of this book first appeared, in part or in their entirety, in the following publications:

"Tijuana Wonderland" in *Many Mountains Moving,* Vol. 2, No. 2 (Spring 1996).

"Down the Highway with Edward Abbey" in *Resist Much, Obey Little: Remembering Ed Abbey,* edited by James

Hepworth and Gregory McNamee (San Francisco: Sierra Club Books, © 1996).

"Whores" in *Muy Macho: Latino Men Confront Their Manhood,* edited by Ray Gonzalez (New York: Anchor Books/ Doubleday, © 1996).

"Leaving Shelltown" in *Hayden's Ferry Review,* Issue 13 (Fall/Winter 1993).

about the author

Luis Alberto Urrea won the American Book Award in 1999 for *Nobody's Son*. He is a best-selling author whose works have appeared in translation around the world. He publishes in several genres—fiction, nonfiction, and poetry. He is the author of several books, among them *The Hummingbird's Daughter*, *The Devil's Highway*, *Across the Wire*, *In Search of Snow*, and *Six Kinds of Sky*. His first book of poetry, *The Fever of Being*, won the Western States Book Award and the Colorado Center for the Book Award. His second poetry collection, *Ghost Sickness*, was represented in *The Best American Poetry of 1996*.

Among his other awards are a Lannan Literary Award, the Kiriyama Pacific Rim Award, and a Christopher Award. He is a member of the Latino Literature Hall of Fame. *The Devil's Highway* was a finalist for the Pulitzer Prize.

Urrea is currently a professor of Creative Writing and Literature at the University of Illinois at Chicago. He lives in the Chicago area with his family. He can be reached at http://www.luisurrea.com.